Georgian Gardens

David C. Stuart

GEORGIAN
GARDENS

Robert Hale

LONDON

ISBN 0 7091 7221 4

Robert Hale Limited
Clerkenwell House
Clerkenwell Green
London, EC1R oHT

Photoset by Jarrold & Sons Ltd,
and printed in Great Britain by
Redwood Burn Ltd, Trowbridge, Wiltshire

Contents

Illustrations

GAZETTEER

Picture Credits

Preface

Any historical book soon comes, in the writing, to owe so much to so many people, that the author is finally at a loss to know whom to thank when it is finished. If I thank only those whose names come immediately to mind, I hope that those not mentioned, who have helped with advice or by their publications, will not be too shocked by my ingratitude. I hope, too, that I will not be haunted by any Georgian author either unacknowledged or ignored.

Firstly, I should like to thank my friends Alma and James Cullen, for it was at their house that the writing of a book on Georgian gardens first seemed possible. Secondly, I must thank the staff of the libraries I have used, especially those of the Royal Botanic Garden, Edinburgh, of the National Library of Scotland, of the Edinburgh Public Library (where Miss Priscilla Minay's enthusiasm often sustained mine) and of the Rare Books Department of the Library of the University of Glasgow (where Mr Jack Baldwin brought my attention to many interesting things). Visual evidence has been quite as important as written, and I should like to thank the staff of a number of archives, including the Print and Drawing Department of the National Gallery of Scotland, the Victoria and Albert Museum, the British Museum and the Royal Institute of British Architects. I should also like to acknowledge the help of the Survey of London, the Archivist of Edinburgh Corporation and the Area Librarian at Bath.

Modern authors to whom my thanks are due may be found in the Bibliography, but I should especially like to draw attention to Miss Blanche Henrey's monumental (and splendid) *British Botanical and Horticultural Literature before 1800*, which appeared during the writing of this work and was of much assistance. It will be of immense use to many others. Of Georgian authors, I cannot help but acknowledge my debt to John Claudius Loudon, whose *Encyclopaedia of Gardening* and *Gardeners' Magazine* have proved veritable treasure troves.

Lastly, I extend my thanks to James Cullen and James Sutherland for reading the manuscript. The former made many useful suggestions and pointed out some glaring botanical errors. The latter kindly restrained some sentences that threatened to take on an independent existence, and coped nobly with my too-justified despondencies and my quite unjustified elations. To them all, my thanks.

David C. Stuart
Edinburgh, 1977

Introduction

"King George . . . set out with the Electoral Prince from Herrenhausen on the thirty-first day of August [1714]; and in five days arrived at The Hague. . . . On the sixteenth day of September he embarked at Orange Poldar, under convoy of an English and Dutch squadron, commanded by the Earl of Berkeley, and next day arrived at The Hope. In the afternoon, the yacht sailed up the river, and His Majesty, with the Prince, were landed from a barge, at Greenwich, about six in the evening." Thus wrote Tobias Smollett in his *History of England*; the Georgian Age had begun.

The exchange of the Hanovers for the Stuarts had no immediate impact on issues so peripheral to the State as garden design, and, in any case, some of the first shots in the revolution of taste in such matters had already been fired. However, no garden in the revolutionary new style had yet been attempted.

The period covered by this book is, in fact, rather shorter than that covered by the reign of the four Georges. It runs from 1730, by which time George II was on the throne, to the death of George IV in 1830. Only by 1730 had the change from the formal gardens of very ancient lineage become inevitable. The new gardens were informal and 'naturalistic', and by 1730 the first few exemplars had been planned and planted. I had hoped, too, that by starting in 1730 I would be absolved from repeating the story of the rise of the landscape garden. This has been often, and often admirably, told by others. The central and last sections of the book do restrict themselves to the original plan. However, I found that in the first section it was impossible to explain the development of garden design (and especially some of its ironies) without describing many things that happened before 1730. I have, though, tried to make as much use as possible of purely gardening sources (which gives the story some new details) and to avoid too much 'art history'. I hope that gardeners will not mind my occasional digressions into architectural matters. My excuse, if one is needed, is that throughout the period theories of design in architecture and gardening were closely related; I hope any architect reader will not find the summaries too crudely done.

I have used the word 'garden' in its very widest sense. Wherever deliberate planting has been carried out, and wherever that planting has been done for its 'looks' (even if at the same time designed for profit), and on whatever scale, it has been regarded as part of the garden. Thus, it includes not only the flower garden and the pleasure ground but the kitchen garden, wilderness, deer park and even, in some rather specialized cases, forest and agricultural land. Each of these aspects of the garden (except for the remarkably conservative, but very interesting, kitchen garden) has played an important part in the rise and fall of the British landscape garden; each aspect has at some point in the story become the dominant one. My aim has been not only to describe this cycle in taste but to give as much of a feeling as I could of the 'reality' of gardens in my chosen hundred years: of the way they were planted, of the plants in them, of the ways in which they were used and enjoyed, and of the way in which they were created and maintained. I hope that gardeners interested in the history of their hobby (or obsession) will find that the first two sections of the book will illumine at least a little of that past and may perhaps provide a few ideas for the future of their own gardens. I hope, too, that they will help to make a visit to any of the Georgian gardens still extant more rewarding, and that it will help to increase their appreciation of them as much as the writing of it has done mine.

The final section, as well as being a general description of the interesting and almost undocumented urban and suburban gardens, lists many larger ones attached to country houses. All of these were, or still are, important or very beautiful examples of various aspects of Georgian gardening. I have tried to concentrate as much as possible on gardens that remain without too much later alteration, and which are open to the public. I have, however, had to include a number that no longer exist, as well as some that, even if now at the full pitch of their beauty, are still completely private. Space and time have not permitted a very extensive documentation. I am well aware that even the longest of the descriptions is woefully inadequate. However, I hope that even the shortest will give the reader a basic context in which to place the garden and, if he can visit it, a little increase in his enjoyment.

1. The revolution accomplished

By 1730, the great revolution in garden design was almost accomplished. Since the fall of the Roman Empire, garden design had been seen in terms of symmetry, control and formalism. Of course, the revolution taking place in England in 1730 did not achieve immediate and total success. Although the great formal terraces of Powis Castle were finished in that year, the magnificent gardens at Bramham, with their straight canals and avenues (the latter radiating from points known as *pattes d'oie*) with vistas and cascades, were still under construction. Indeed, they were not finished until the 1750s, the same decade that work at last stopped on the avenues and flat lawns of St Paul's Walden Bury and on the splendid gardens of Newliston near Edinburgh. However, in 1730 the wealthy Lord Burlington's old Tudor house at Chiswick was pulled down, and the new landscape around the new villa was nearly complete. Alexander Pope's five-acre garden at Twickenham was finished, and widely admired. The artist and designer William Kent had just begun work on the gardens at Claremont and Stowe, and at Stowe the village (the first of many) had just been swept away, its foundations invisible beneath a sweep of new green lawn.

These new gardens were believed by their fond owners and admirers to be the mirror of Nature, all earlier gardens to be distortions of it. Of the then new gardens that still remain (Pope's garden was destroyed by Lord Stanhope soon after Pope's death), more than two hundred years of growth have filled them with massive trees and natural-looking vegetation. It is difficult now to imagine how they looked when first planted. Their designer, of course, planned for maturity, but the hundreds of contemporary views published as prints, and avidly bought by the public, naturally wished to flatter both garden and owner, so they almost always show the vegetation with a vigour and luxuriance it cannot by then have had. Interesting though these prints are, the most useful way of appreciating how these early informal gardens looked is to examine their plans. Pope's gardener, John Serle, published a plan of that garden in 1745. Plans of Burlington's

Chiswick garden appeared in 1736. In spite of the claims made for them, by their owners and by subsequent historians, these gardens still had remarkably strong formal elements. There were still straight walks or *allées*, still edged with clipped hawthorn or box hedges. Water was still held in straight canals, tumbled over marble cascades or was pumped through the nozzles of fountains. In the light of what gardens were to become in only a few years, the changes seem minor. In the 'wildernesses' behind the straight hedges, the trees were neither pruned nor pleached, and meandering paths joined glade to glade. In some, ponds had wavy margins, and grass and water joined without a formal boundary of stone. More rarely, water ran in channels mimicking the appearance of natural streams and waterfalls. Over the following century, it was these elements that were to preoccupy garden designers, while avenues and canals vanished, it was believed, forever.

Although various explanations have been put forward for this revolution, and although many forces later propelled it towards its final extinction, one of the most powerful urges in its initiation was that to re-create the gardens of ancient Rome. Since the Renaissance the Roman world had been a source of speculation and fascination, but, before the eighteenth century, little attention had been paid to Roman gardens. The garden at Chiswick was begun in 1725, the same year that saw the publication of Richard Bradley's *Survey of the Ancient Husbandry and Gardening . . . collected from Cato, Varro, Columella, Virgil . . . and other Greeks and Romans.* Bradley often compares the rather vague descriptions of ancient gardens in an unfavourable way with the gardens of early-eighteenth-century England. Noting the formal parterres of Rome, he says that modern times have hardly shown an improvement; indeed, the current regularity, "however well it may appear on a paper design, is stiff and surfeiting when it came to be put into execution. In our modern designs we see all at once, and lose the pleasure of expectation; fine irregular plots of ground, which in themselves had ten thousand beauties, are brought to a level at an immense expense, and then give us so little amusement that the change is generally regretted, and the spirit of gardening . . . sinks." Later, using both the ancient sources and rumours of Lord Burlington's project, he writes: "We might have grottoes and caves disposed in a rustic manner, and at certain points of view obelisks might be placed, or summer houses or pavilions built after the manner of Grecian temples, to be planted about with fir trees. . . ." As he then goes on to "treat of the methods used by the ancients for the education of Fowls", we can leave him there, noting how much his description can be applied to the gardens at Chiswick or Twickenham. Bradley's suggestion that "we might still improve these agreeables [natural hills and valleys] if we were to borrow so much from the Versailles gardens as we might take in at small expense . . ." was not taken up, for he would have added the "Fables of

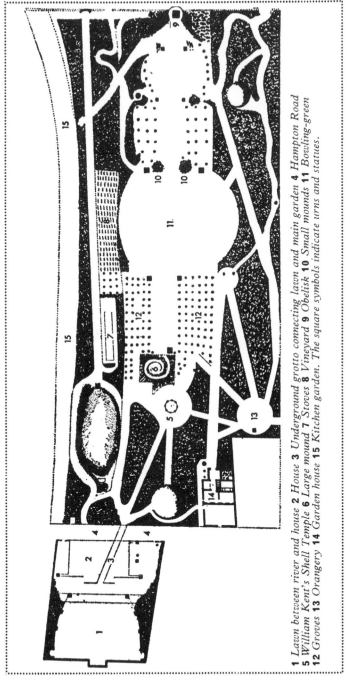

1 *Lawn between river and house* 2 *House* 3 *Underground grotto connecting lawn and main garden* 4 *Hampton Road*
5 *William Kent's Shell Temple* 6 *Large mound* 7 *Stoves* 8 *Vineyard* 9 *Obelisk* 10 *Small mounds* 11 *Bowling-green*
12 *Groves* 13 *Orangery* 14 *Garden house* 15 *Kitchen garden. The square symbols indicate urns and statues.*

Serle's plan of Alexander Pope's garden: formal elements predominate, especially the central
axis. The winding walks are peripheral to the main garden.

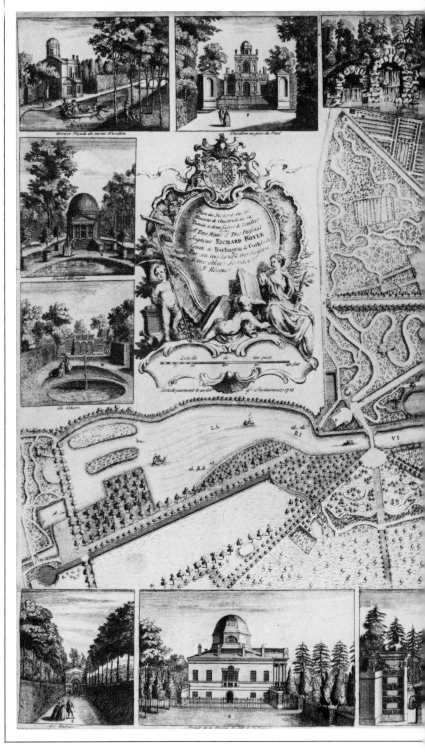

Roque's plan of Chiswick shows the strong formal elements that remain in the proto-landscape garden.

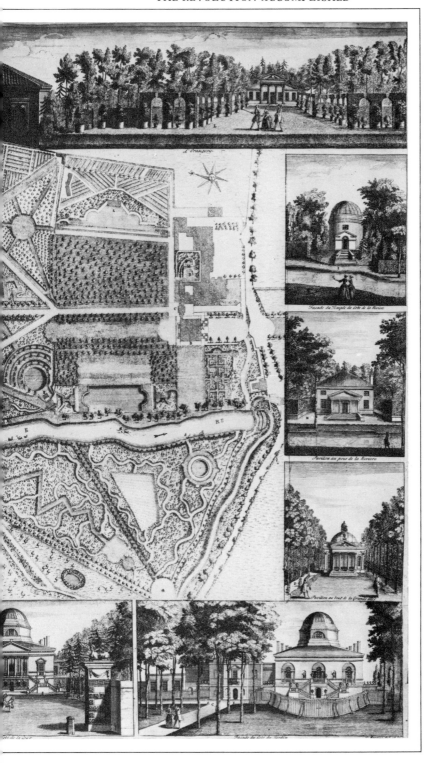

Aesop", life-sized and life-coloured, scattered through the wilderness. Lord Burlington would not have approved.

In 1728 another important attempt at the reconstruction of Roman gardens was published. Robert Castell's *Villas of the Ancients*, based largely on the letters of Pliny the Younger, shows the highly speculative reconstructions only as plans. Until the first discovery of frescoes at Herculaneum and Pompeii later in the century, no one knew much about the elevations of the Romans' private houses, and less about their gardens. Castell, and his patrons, following earlier practice, still saw the 'plan' as the most essential element in garden, and house, design. In any case, Castell's plans are almost indistinguishable from those of Chiswick and Twickenham. As Burlington had supported the book's production, it is difficult to disentangle flattery from a genuine archaeological attempt. The only exotic elements found in Rome, but not near London, were the areas of garden set aside for the breeding of snails and dormice, neither animal playing any part in eighteenth-century gastronomy.

The year 1728 also saw the production of another influential work, Batty Langley's *New Principles of Gardening*, and although it paid little attention to ancient Rome, only a few of his suggestions now seem especially naturalistic (perhaps the book sold on the title alone). The wilderness was to be of "shady walks and groves, planted with sweet briar, white jessamine and honeysuckle, environed at the bottom with a small circle of dwarf stock, candytuft and pinks". Lawns were to be decorated with trellis obelisks covered with passion-flowers, more honeysuckle, jasmine and grapes. However, he does say that "the end and design of a good garden is to be both profitable and delightful, wherein should be observed that the parts should always be presenting new objects, which is a continual entertainment to the eye, and raises a pleasure of imagination."

Langley, Bradley and Castell were all writers closely associated with these new proto-landscape gardens; they themselves were influenced by (and Langley plagiarized) several writers of the first two decades of the century. Of these, Stephen Switzer was the most fully concerned with gardening. His *Ichnographia Rustica* . . . of 1718 contains many splendid things; some of the garden plans, although showing straight avenues and canals, do also have some of the first illustrated serpentine walks and streams. Of these, he says: "We must cashier that mathematical stiffness in our gardens, and imitate Nature more." He disliked the earlier clipped trees and bushes, "when, in truth, the loose tresses of a tree or plant, that is easily fanned by every gentle breeze of air, and the natural though unpolished dress of a beautiful field, lawn or meadow [is] much more entertaining than the utmost exactitude of the most finished parterre, and curiosest interlacings of box work or embroidery". Switzer's gardens (and he designed many) also show an awareness of the larger landscape beyond the garden. Of course, earlier walled gardens had had ironwork grilles, or mounts, from which to see the outside world. But Switzer emphasizes that the wilderness and surrounding woods should be opened up, especially "when you have blue hills, a fine valley or some noble lawn, tower or rising hills, clothed with wood at a large distance. These are features so noble that even a grown wood ought to be cut down to admit an open view to it." The whole estate, he thinks, should be both beautiful and productive, with its waters teeming with carp, the rides and plantations abounding with pheasants, partridges and hares, and the hedges planted with fruit trees and filberts.

While Switzer's ideas on naturalism undoubtedly owed something to Addison and Temple, whom we shall meet in a moment, and more deeply to the philosopher Lord Shaftesbury (who receives fuller treatment in the next chapter), his strongly felt opinion that an estate should be economically integrated is his own. Certainly, in 1718, with Britain still unsure of the permanence of the new dynasty, still exhausted by the foreign wars of William and Anne and continually troubled by the rising strife between Whig and Tory at home, few landowners can have had sufficient confidence in the future to embark on the production of the vast baroque gardens still fashionable on the Continent, and once fashionable in England. These were almost exclusively for show; great houses sat like spiders at the confluence of immense avenues whose only function was ceremony or to speed the chase, and whose only logical termination was another great house. In fact, most of these avenues simply petered out in open country, though Blenheim, Ditchley and Heythrop were once linked by such a system. This unproductive grandeur can no longer have seemed sensible. Further, these 'French' gardens had become firmly associated with the Stuart dynasty, with their doubtful allegiance to the English Church, their connection with, and envy of, the French monarchy, and indeed, as symbols of their hankerings for absolute power. Surprisingly, the Hanovers paid little attention to the new garden style (with which they could so easily have associated themselves), with its virtuous combination of pleasure and utility, and its redolence of British patriotism. Perhaps the memory of their own splendid and formal garden at Herrenhausen was too strong. No Hanoverian, until Frederick Lewis, Prince of Wales (d. 1751), played any part in the development of garden design.

Stephen Switzer seems to have been responsible for the extensive hydraulic system of Wray Wood begun at Castle Howard in 1718. The original intention had been to continue the formal Broad Walk straight up through the plantation. Switzer, who had published extensively on the ways of making fountains and cascades, was called in to produce them among the winding walks that were cut through the trees. Wray Wood is not the only very early naturalistic element at Castle Howard; the walk to the splendid

Castell's reconstruction of Pliny's garden at Laurentium: it shows strong
similarities to the Chiswick plan.

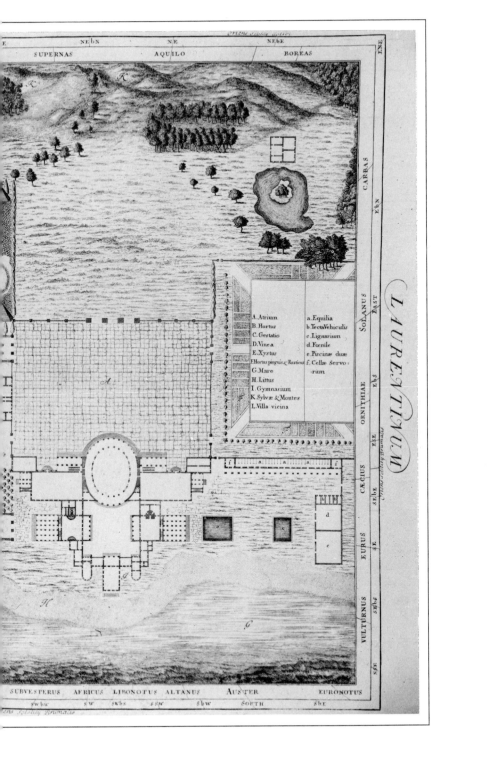

LAURENTINUM

A. Atrium	a. Equilia
B. Hortus	b. Tecta Vehiculis
C. Gestatio	c. Lignarium
D. Vinea	d. Foenile
E. Xystus	e. Pucinæ duæ
F. Hortus pinguis & Rusticus	f. Cellæ Servorum
G. Mare	
H. Littus	
I. Gymnasium	
K. Sylvæ & Montes	
L. Villa vicina	

Temple of the Winds (its interior decoration planned in 1730) follows the line of an old lane, although formally punctuating it with statuary. Vanbrugh had also hoped to produce some landscape elements at Blenheim, with the retention of the ancient Woodstock Manor as an eye-catcher. His hopes were defeated, and Blenheim was not landscaped until Brown worked there later in the century.

Of the writers who influenced Switzer, Addison (a founder and frequent contributor to the *Spectator* and *Tatler*) had his own beloved estate at Bilston. Although a number of straight walks and avenues still remain, there were informal parts (described on page 68). In 1710, he wrote, "The mind of Man naturally hates everything that looks like restraint upon it, and is apt to fancy itself under a sort of confinement when the sight is pent up in a narrow compass, or shortened on every side by the neighbourhood of walls or mountains." Later, he described a splendid, and wall-less, ideal garden that had "rocks shaped into artificial grottoes covered with woodbines and jessamines [Batty Langley's honeysuckles and jasmines] . . . the woods are cut into shady walks . . . the springs are made to run among pebbles . . . collected into a beautiful lake that is inhabited by a couple of swans . . . which empties itself by a little rivulet which runs through a green meadow."

Sir William Temple took a rather different position. H⁻ designed his own garden to be unashamedly formal, but it was a conscious anachronism, being a copy of a garden he had much admired as a young man. Indeed, he called his own house by the same name, Moor Park. But in discussing Chinese gardens, he did admit that irregular gardens could also be beautiful, even if they would be very difficult to do well. The engraving of his Moor Park by Jan Kip (about 1708) shows a meandering and artificial watercourse, so perhaps Temple had experimented.

With the fall from favour of baroque gardens, came a fall in baroque architecture. The reasons were similar and of the same date. Baroque houses were seen as pompous and rhetorical, atrociously expensive to build and designed more for ceremony than habitation. The visual language that began to replace the baroque was also compounded of the same elements: Rome and patriotism. Lord Burlington, too, was deeply concerned in the new movement. The neglected architect who was discovered to combine Britishness with a pure, chaste and Roman style was Inigo Jones. Jones had visited Italy several times and had been deeply impressed by the writings, drawings and buildings of the sixteenth-century architect Andrea Palladio. Palladio had made many measured drawings of Roman antiquities (then more numerous than they are today) and had also studied the writings of the fourth-century Roman architect Vitruvius. Lord Burlington started, almost single-handed, a Palladian revival. Although much of the information on which the new architectural language was based was later found to be misinterpreted, or even incorrect, he and his friends felt that they had a secure key to the beauties of ancient Rome. Ignoring the fact that Palladio's houses were set in rigidly formal gardens, they had a much less sure key to the beauties of ancient gardens. All must have realized that neither Castell nor Bradley could offer enough. Garden designers turned to other aspects of Italian culture.

2. Italy

The world of ancient Rome has almost always exerted a powerful appeal to men unfortunate enough to have been born after its fall. Even Theodoric the Ostrogoth attempted the restoration of parts of the city in A.D. 510, only a hundred years after its sack by Alaric. Even by then parts of it were too decayed to make repair worth while. For the following five or six hundred years, the ancient city became merely a quarry for building materials, but at the beginning of the Renaissance men once again began to speculate about that astonishing city and the state of which it had been the centre. Its authors and playwrights were once again read and enjoyed, and its standards of visual beauty appreciated. Further, beyond these productions of a powerful and very complex culture were glimpses of the more cerebral achievements of Greece. The new belief in the power and necessity of the human mind to explore every aspect of creation spread rapidly through Europe. The intellectual possibilities travelled more quickly than the associated visual ones; classical elements derived from Roman buildings first appear in England, usually clustered incorrectly together, on the fronts of Elizabethan houses that are otherwise thoroughly romantic. It was 1630 before the first correctly classical building appeared in England, fifty years after the death of Andrea Palladio: it was 'the Queen's House' at Greenwich, by Inigo Jones.

Naturally, an interest in ancient Rome led noblemen and wealthy merchants to collect Roman artefacts. Popes and princes had already begun to collect statues, columns and other architectural fragments for the decoration of their new palaces and gardens. One of the first English collections was formed by the Earl of Arundel. It was begun in 1613, when he was twenty-five, when he went to Italy in company with Jones. Jones, then forty, spoke fluent Italian and on this journey travelled with his own copy of Palladio's *Four Books of architecture*. (This book, crammed with Jones's notes, was later to be in Burlington's collection, as were, after remarkable vicissitudes, fragments of the Arundel Marbles.) Although the new classical style promulgated by Jones was embodied in a few marvellous buildings, after his death in 1652 it was hardly followed. It was too advanced for those who still adhered to the indigenous British style, and, on the other hand, it was not advanced enough for younger architects and patrons who could see the architecture of contemporary Italy moving into the exhilarating movement and theatricality of the baroque. Nevertheless, although architects themselves might lose interest in the appearance of ancient, rather than modern, Rome, their patrons did not. They continued to travel to Italy in increasing numbers, and the 'Grand Tour' became an institution among all rich and idle young men in search of pleasure or education. It remained so until the end of the eighteenth century. The major Italian cities were full of English rich, of guides to historical sites and Italian Society (poor gentlemen could buy guide-books only for the former), full of pimps and parasites, antique-dealers and picture-dealers. The decorative spoils were shipped back to England. Statues, funerary urns, bas-reliefs, coins, plates, fragments of buildings and furniture, left from every port in Italy. The Roman clutter passing through British Customs varied in quality from the most chipped and tawdry relics to some of the most supreme masterpieces of Roman art. Their proud, and often uncritical, owners housed their treasures in cabinets, loggias or vast sculpture galleries, all belonging to houses that at least tried to emulate, sometimes even surpassed, Roman magnificence. However, as well as these fragments of an ancient civilization, many of these travellers brought back modern Italian paintings and, more importantly for the development of garden design, Italian landscape paintings of the sixteenth century.

Anthony Ashley Cooper, third Earl of Shaftesbury, first visited Italy in 1686, by which time the four most important landscape painters were dead. Lord Shaftesbury was not well-off, indeed he eventually lived in Italy both for preference and from financial prudence. Although he, too, would have liked to buy fine paintings of historical subjects by Guido Reni, the Caracci and the rest, he wrote home to his friends that such *genre* had become so expensive that landscape paintings were the only, and much cheaper, alternative. In English houses landscapes were so little valued that they were generally hung over doors or chimney-pieces.

However much Shaftesbury was a champion of modern Italian painting, the philosophical ideas of the ancient world were of deeper fascination. He was a humanist, and his personal philosophy was a fusion of the Stoic and the Platonic. He attacked the idea of original sin, of the Fall and of Satan. He found 'nature' transformed from a dark and fallen world trying to achieve order and perfection (Eden presumably having parterres) into a revelation of innate goodness and beauty. Nature, though, meant more to him than simply the unpruned trees of the hedgerow or the reedy margins of the stream. Following the idea of the Platonic 'essence', it meant nature at its most ideal, as representing the very highest sorts of beauty, truth and goodness. His passion for these qualities was intense and had in it a touch of the puritanical. In *Second Characters* he could write that, "In true moral philosophy, as in painting, the truly austere, severe and regular restraintive character . . . corresponds (not fights or thwarts) with the free, the easy, the secure, the bold . . . ." He explained the presence of pain, ugliness and deformity by the smallness of human vision but, unable himself to be detached, had an intense dislike of distorted and artificial forms. In gardening he found these associated with the extravagant show that was the result of self-aggrandizement. He died before the Baroque was vanquished by the harmonious and restrained buildings of the Palladians, and never saw the early landscapes that surrounded them. He believed (and they followed) that true beauty, and its related qualities, was the result of the creative re-assembly of elements in the external world by the mind of man. It is this idea that found expression in the writings of Addison and Switzer. Shaftesbury published little that related specifically to gardening, but, as we have seen, his philosophy gave ample reason for the rejection of the earlier formal style. Neither Addison, Switzer, Pope nor the proto-landscapes provided a visual language for gardening that fully matched it. Shaftesbury discovered it when he bought Italian landscape paintings.

By the early decades of the eighteenth century all landscape paintings were eagerly bought. Of the Italians, the most valuable of all were by four men: Nicolas Poussin, Caspar Dughet (also known as Caspar Poussin), Claude Lorrain and Salvator Rosa. All four were constantly invoked in discussions on landscape design until well into the nineteenth century. All four men had very different styles and personalities, and it is not fanciful to identify these differences with quite distinctive currents in the development of taste in landscape and garden design until formalism in gardens reasserted itself. It is also worth pointing out that the works of all these men were known to a far wider public than those fortunate enough to own the originals. Many of the paintings were extensively copied (there were also many fakes), and all were in wide circulation as engravings which were, and still are, avidly collected. It soon became fashionable to allude to any landscape, whether Thames-side meadow or Alpine cliff, in terms of one or other of the painters. It became so general, as did the claim to 'taste' in such matters, that it is hard to believe that the correct painter was invoked for the appropriate view. Claude Lorrain's style became so much the rage that his name was even taken for a piece of optical equipment indispensable to any eighteenth-century tourist. The 'Claude glass' was a slightly convex mirror cut into a square four inches by three and a half. It was used to view the landscape, but, as it was only weakly silvered, the landscape appeared darkened and romanticized, as if seen through a darkened glaze. It was certainly a cheaper alternative to that used by the amateur painter Sir Charles Beaumont. He,

Caspar Dughet's charming Arcadias provided models for landscape in the eighteenth century and for Italianate cottages in the nineteenth.

'Solitude', by Poussin, perhaps the most influential artist of the *genre* and one of the most Romantic.

'Landscape with Mercury and the Dishonest Woodman': Salvator Rosa's paintings often showed a darker side to landscape and human nature.

'The marriage of Isaac and Rebekah' (sometimes called 'The Mill'), by Claude.

lucky man, always took a genuine Claude with him on painting trips to ensure that his colour values were correct (by the painting, that is, not the real landscape).

Lord Shaftesbury, with his belief in the moral value of beauty, in restraint and proportion, was perhaps most attracted by the paintings of Poussin. Although Poussin painted no pure landscapes until late in his life, when he did, they contained the same stern architectural quality and clearly worked out composition as his historical work. Incidentally, the backgrounds of these, when they are anything other than a plain wall, often show landscapes containing buildings of a geometrical purity not attempted until the neo-classical architects of one hundred and fifty years later aspired to 'the Sublime'. Most of his works were produced in the studio, where he had time to reach the essence of the events or scenes depicted. The colouring is never allowed to invoke wonder or sensuous enjoyment. In gardening terms, Poussin represents the elevation of reason, function and morality.

Caspar Dughet, his brother-in-law, had a remarkably different approach; indeed, one wonders if the two men can possibly have liked one another. Dughet started as a full-time painter of landscapes in 1630 and was immediately successful, both artistically and commercially. He was much less concerned with Platonic ideas of essences and with the moral and intellectual content of his paintings. Significantly, he worked from the real landscape in the open air, concerned with the fleeting beauties of nature rather than the eternal. There are few classical ruins in his paintings; what buildings there are are the farmhouses and cottages of the contemporary inhabitants. Consequently, there is little feeling of the weight of the past. With his less introspective and more sensual nature (he was also passionately fond of hunting and dogs), it is perhaps not surprising that he was a very successful designer for the theatre and even saw nothing demeaning in employment decorating the cases of harpsichords. Engravings were made from his paintings from the end of the seventeenth century, and some instantly show some of the origins of the new 'English garden'. Dughet may be identified with what was to be a very strong element in British gardening, and one which had been almost the foundation of baroque gardens: the garden seen as theatre or as the setting for a masque.

In the paintings of Salvator Rosa, intellect, tranquillity, sometimes even beauty, are subjugated to violence and sensation. The landscape is composed of peaks and chasms, waterfalls, torrents, great trees seared by storm or fire. The population, dwarfed by their surroundings, are either vagabonds or bandits. His paintings were enormously popular throughout the eighteenth century, and his style was emulated by many artists. He must have appealed to anyone who found life too tame and the formal conventions of society too constricting; indeed, he developed a posthumous reputation for being wild, solitary, extravagant, of frequently consorting with the sort of people in his paintings, and even worse. He was a revolutionary, a word with a very bad, and a very exciting, odour, especially at the end of the eighteenth century. His qualities became of particular importance from mid-century, with the rise of the gothic movement in literature and architecture, and rather later in gardening.

Rosa was by no means a major painter. However, the last of the quartet, Claude Lorrain, was then, and still is, considered a master. Living and working in Rome for most of his life, he was immensely productive and widely patronized at the highest levels of society. His works were so sought after, and so often faked, that in 1635 he began to compile the *Liber Veritatis* (*Book of Truth*), which contained his own drawings of all the paintings that he had produced. The drawings themselves are often of the greatest beauty, and the collection was in the possession of the Dukes of Devonshire by 1728. While Claude did some sketches from nature, the paintings were mostly produced in the studio, yet they contain a marvellous feeling for the countryside around Rome and Naples. The combination of vegetation and architecture (usually the overgrown ruins of Roman or medieval building) is peopled more or less equally with figures from Roman or Christian myth. All have a very strong feeling for the past, but it is a mood (lyrical, nostalgic, often deeply peaceful) not an intellectual attempt at correctness or historical re-creation. Only rarely does a sinister element add a piquant note to the softly lit landscapes. Claude's paintings were perhaps the most influential of all, and many of the English Arcadias of the mid eighteenth century may be seen as attempts to create their mood, whatever the underlying reasons and however passionate may have been the argument about the means.

3. Sets, scenery and sentiment

With the increasing awareness that these four landscape painters could provide the language for a new style in gardening, it is not surprising that a living painter played a decisive role in the language's development. Earlier, in 1705, Vanbrugh's call for a landscape painter to design the gardens at Blenheim had been ignored. No painter had a hand in landscape design until the momentous advent of William Kent. Aged forty in 1730, he had spent a number of years in Italy in his youth, first seeing that country in 1713. He had been deeply affected by its culture; even his personal mannerisms had become so Italianate (a not uncommon phenomenon since at least Shakespeare's England) that he was known, perhaps not affectionately, as the 'Signor'. He had been sent out, financed by a number of minor Yorkshire gentlemen, to study great paintings in order to become a great painter. Study he did, copying among much else a number of paintings by Lorrain (he eventually owned several Poussins and Rosas), but he never became a great painter. At best he was second rate. Nevertheless, Italy provided him with an eye for paintings, architecture and interior decoration, and also with a patron rich enough to develop and exploit those talents, fitful but sometimes approaching major, that he had. The patron was Lord Burlington, and Kent's talents were for building and landscape design.

Kent has often been hailed as the father of the English landscape. Horace Walpole was perhaps the earliest exponent of this view, and it is worth quoting him at some length:

> At that moment [after Bridgeman's use of the ha-ha had enabled garden and countryside to seem continuous] appeared Kent, painter enough to taste the charms of landscape, bold and opinionative enough to dare and to dictate, and born with a genius to strike out a great system from the twilight of imperfect essays. He leapt the fence and saw that all nature was a garden . . . . Thus the pencil of his imagination bestowed all the arts of landscape on the scenes he handled. The great principles on which he worked were perspective, and light and shade . . . [and] he realized the compositions of the greatest masters in

Kent's designs for Holkham show architectural similarities with Batty Langley, but with self-consciously irregular planting.

painting. Where objects were wanting to animate his horizon, his taste as an architect could bestow immediate termination. His buildings, his seats, his temples, were more the works of his pencil than of his compasses. We owe the restoration of Greece and the diffusion of architecture to his skill in landscape.

But of all the beauties that he added to the face of this beautiful country, none surpasses his management of water. Adieu to canals, circular basons and cascades tumbling down marble steps . . . . The forced elevation of cataracts was no more. The gentle stream was taught to serpentize seemingly at its pleasure, and where discontinued at different levels, its course appeared to be concealed by thickets properly interspersed, and glittered again at a distance where it might be supposed naturally to arrive.

However, it is not quite as simple as that. Kent had certainly been involved in the formation of the proto-landscape at Chiswick and of the Elysian Fields at Stowe. The garden at Rousham, begun by Kent in 1738, for General Dormer (the only Kent garden to survive very much as designed), is not a proto-landscape; it is a landscape garden in a much fuller sense. Of course, it was not only Kent who had changed. Britain itself had undergone a considerable metamorphosis, and one which affected gardens as considerably as the developments of Kent's thinking.

By the late 1730s the new dynasty was at last felt to be reasonably secure, and many political and constitutional problems seemed near resolution. New export markets were forming in America and the West Indies, Asia and Africa. Manufacturers were becoming rich. In spite of the increasing pace of economic activity (partly stimulated by war), the decade was also one of agricultural depression. Profits from land had been low for many years (or perhaps baroque gardens would never have been so vast) but were decreasing. Farmers and small landowners became poorer, and many were finally forced to sell. The wealthy, whether urban or already landed, and those whose dependence on their income was rather more flexible, found that they could buy land very cheaply. New estates were formed; large estates became larger, and owners of scattered estates could consolidate their holdings at a single centre. Throughout the decade it must have seemed natural for the newly landed to create gardens in the latest fashion. This was being set by the great Whig magnates, with all of whom William Kent was associated.

Although the early landscapes of 1730 can best be seen as two-dimensional ground-plans, and in this way similar to everything that had gone before, Kent's training as a painter predisposed him to see gardens still in two dimensions, but vertically, as in a picture or a theatre set, rather than horizontally. Once this change had taken place, the way was open for the disappearance of all remaining formal elements in the design, and for the expansion of the wilderness.

Kent seems to have been an expansive and exuberant man, with a taste for

An Arbor in a
Fortified Island

Plate XVIII.

Tho: Bowles Sculp.

Frontispieces of Trelliss Work for the enterances, into Temples of View. Arbors, Shady walks &c.

French-looking trellis pavilions advocated by Batty Langley in *New Principles of Gardening*.

Suggested designs for canvas flats to be put at the ends of vistas – Batty Langley, *New Principles of Gardening*.

good living and theatre, and at times temperamental and superficial. His patron was his complete antithesis. Even in architecture, while Kent could switch style at once from Palladian to gothic or Chinese, Burlington pursued his narrow ideal of Roman purity. Kent's buildings were generally well planned and comfortable; Burlington's obsession with façade and symmetry often conflicted with both functions, and with the owner's needs (General Wade discovered that he had no wallspace on which to hang the pictures for which he had had the house designed). One can perhaps see an affinity with Poussin in Burlington, and with Caspar Dughet (and possibly with Claude) in Kent; the Kentian garden as a set for a play or masque, as something to see oneself and one's friends in, and in which effect is more important than the purity of means; the Burlingtonian garden as a unity composed of intellect, restraint, even a certain suppression of the more chaotic elements in human nature.

While this latter type became important after 1750, the 'theatre' garden had already germinated in Batty Langley's book of 1728. There, he suggests that vistas (straight ones in 1728) may be terminated, if there is no real view or solid building, by a painted canvas 'flat' like a theatre backdrop, and he gives several illustrations. Many were actually built, but I know of no surviving examples. Even in spite of later changes in taste, theatricalities kept appearing, and in 1784 Truseler's *Elements of Modern Gardening* suggests that "a stable, a barn or a brew-house, faced with timber or plaster, may be made to represent a temple, a ruin or a cottage; and at a distance, or out of reach of discovery, a painting may be substituted for a bridge over a piece of water. . . ." A well-known example of such fraudulent practice is the flat cut-out bridge over the end of the lake at Kenwood. Even at the height of revulsion against such fakery at the beginning of the honest nineteenth century, when even pagan temples were frowned upon, John Claudius Loudon could calmly suggest that gardeners should tie artificial flowers and tiny bottles of scent in unflowering bushes if employers or guests were expected at an unpromising time of the year.

Horace Walpole was very conscious of the self-aware and masque-like use of gardens when he wrote, in May 1763, of a fête of Miss Pelham's at Claremont (by then altered from Kent's original layout):

> We walked to the belvedere on the summit of the hill, where a theatrical show only served to heighten the beauty of the landscape, a rainbow on a dark cloud falling precisely behind the tower of a neighbouring church, and the building at Claremont. . . . From thence we passed into the wood, and the ladies formed a circle on chairs before the mouth of a cave, which was overhung to a vast height with woodbines, lilacs and laburnums, and dignified with tall stately cypresses. On the descent of the hill were placed French horns; the abigails, servants and neighbours wandering below by the river; in short, it was Parnassus, as Watteau would have painted it.

Physical theatricality in gardens also had an emotional counterpart: an intense sentimentality. Although, as we shall see, much of this was attached to garden building and ornament, Salvator Rosa's paintings for those who stayed at home, and the Alpine crossing for those who journeyed to Italy, were primarily responsible. Feelings of awe and wonder are entirely justified by the wilder manifestations of the natural world, but such feelings became absurd when they were attached to the generally much less spectacular English landscape or, worse, to the attempted landscapes of English gardens. A circle of hillocks were imagined to be the hills of Tuscany after Poussin, and anything larger than a babbling brook was seen as a torrent out of Salvator Rosa.

For instance, The Leasowes was much visited and applauded (even by Walpole) in the middle of the century. It was visited by William Marshall in 1785, by which time sentimental fashions had changed. Of it, Marshall wrote, after his description of crossing one of the torrents, "We should probably have crossed this unnoticed, had it not been for a dirty little obelisk, bearing a Latin inscription, and a few seats which are scattered here and there in what, if we recollect rightly, is named 'Virgil's Grove'." He goes on, after noting that one of the small valleys had been dammed to make a reservoir and a cascade about ten feet in height, that "Unfortunately however, for Art, she could not augment the stream, which is naturally much too slender to give full effect to this ingenious device, sacred we understood, to Venus. This cascade only plays occasionally, and we arrived at an uninteresting moment." Later, in another part of the garden, the caretaker turned on the waters for Marshall and his companion, and "at length, the water gushed out from among some large roots of a tree, falling five or six feet perpendicular; presently we saw it falling down another *precipice*, and [then] another, until my companion was in ecstasy. . . . 'Very pretty, upon my word!' And pray, is not the cascade of tin and horsebeans at Vauxhall very pretty? *Quaere*, did Vauxhall copy after The Leasowes, or The Leasowes after Vauxhall?" Marshall, with his love of horses and women, his interest in forestry and rural economy, his sense of 'scale' in landscape, and his dislike of paganism, cannot be expected to be in sympathy with Shenstone, the watery bachelor and bad poet who owned The Leasowes.

For Stowe, Rousham and the other gardens, Kent designed some superb garden buildings. While many of these were intended to have various associations (Temples of Ancient Virtue, Modern Virtue – in ruins, Concorde, Venus, even Priapus), less wealthy garden-owners who could not employ first-rate architects nevertheless loaded garden ornaments with similar sentiments. Kent's pavilions gave a Roman ambience to gardens: a general feel of Augustan gravity and grandeur. The range of emotional intention of the myriad lesser ornaments was far wider. Urns (all derived from Roman funerary monuments) were to induce melancholy thoughts on death and the transitoriness of earthly pleasures. Obelisks shared a similar function (both Pope and Shenstone had ones dedicated to their mothers; Walpole, also a bachelor, seems to have been less concerned). Obelisks could also commemorate battles of ancient times and were thus classical cousins to the ruined gothic castle, also intended to invoke meditation on departed might. Hermitages were for another sort of medieval melancholy, a species of sentimental 'other worldliness' no doubt induced by the surrounding displays of material wealth and pomp.

Hermitages had a remarkably long career, and remarkably varied architectural expression. The sentimental hermit could take his, or her, pick from artificial caves, sophisticated plaster-gothic pavilions or cottages built of roots and moss. Few were seriously habitable; some had waxwork divines with the obligatory books, hourglass and skull beside them. A number of wealthy proprietors did, however, try to hire full-time hermits. The post was often well paid, food provided from the house, but hermits were expected never to speak, to cut their hair or fingernails, or even to wash. Celibacy was, of course, essential. No hermit seems to have survived the ordeal for very long, all soon succumbing to the bottle or the milkmaids.

Even the humble garden seat, so necessary when a garden could have several miles of walks, was inscribed with lines of poetry, pointing up either the scenes of rural interest available to the spectator, or the sorrows and miseries of unhappy love. Each of these locations in the garden was meant to intensify an already existing feeling, where this was possible. Where it was not, then they had to induce such a feeling in those who, perhaps through the boredom of country-house living, felt nothing. Such was the enthusiasm for these second-hand excitements that a walk around the pleasure garden must have been emotionally quite exhausting.

Behind the advanced theoreticians and patrons followed slowly the rest of the gardening world. Philip Miller, one of the most famous gardeners of the age, published the 1739 edition of his *Gardeners' Dictionary* with a half-hearted apology that the 1731 edition had still advocated formalism in gardens. The 1739 edition describes how modern gardens were created by

> opening walks through the different parts, which may be twisted about after an easy natural manner, so as to show as little of Art as possible. If to this is added some large openings, in such places where there are few good trees, which may be varied in their figures [plans] and some little buildings, obelisks, vases, urns, etc., placed properly in them, it will add greatly to their magnificence. . . .
>
> In laying out these walks through woods there should be a great regard had to the neighbouring country, so as wherever there are any distant objects which appear to the sight, there should be openings to which the serpentine walks should lead, from whence the objects may be viewed, which will be an agreeable surprise to strangers after having traversed through many of these

walks, to be led to a fine prospect of the adjacent country, where a village, church or some other remarkable object may appear to the sight, or perhaps a river or other large body of water. . . .

By the time this was written, advanced taste was ready to move on. By mid-century the proto-landscape had given way to a new style, one in which crude associations of ideas were frowned upon and in which much of the earlier garden paraphernalia was swept away. The garden had now become Arcadia.

4. Arcadia

The impetus that had carried taste so far away from the fashion of earlier centuries did not stop when William Kent had developed the theatrical picture-garden. Like all revolutions, the system of ideas underlying the new style accumulated such momentum that they were carried onwards, beyond Roman precedent, towards a new idiom and eventually to their own destruction. By 1750 Kent had been dead for two years; Lord Burlington was no longer the principal arbiter of taste, and Lancelot Brown (not yet known as 'Capability') had just set himself up in London as a free-lance designer. Brown's name completely dominates the middle period of Georgian landscape design, and indeed it remains today the one most frequently associated with the conventional idea of Georgian gardens. He had rivals, but few achieved any great influence. Perhaps this was a pity; it was the dominance of his strong, particular and unvarying vision of the ideal landscape that caused such a violent reaction to it, and so the demise of the English landscape garden.

The most important contribution that Brown made was the transition from landscape seen in a two-dimensional, if vertical, way to a landscape fully integrated in three dimensions: landscape as sculpture, rather than as painting. It was a landscape meant to be moved through and observed the whole time, not one in which to sit down at pre-selected points and observe the composition. As well as this new integration, Brown also reduced, sometimes entirely, the number of extraneous elements in the garden. In this purification, obelisks, urns and the rest of the paraphernalia vanished. Removed too were flowerbeds, flower gardens, avenues, terraces, fountains, cascades and grottoes, leaving only a few suitably chaste temples and pavilions. The Brownian landscape was worked out in three elements alone: wood, water and grass. Even the woods were purified, for unnecessary exotics were eschewed, Brown often restricting his planting to eight or nine species, and most of those native. In this reduction to simplicity, indeed this strong stylization of 'nature', Brown represents the Poussinesque aspect of garden design. Further, even the largest proto-landscapes and Kentian gardens were all built up from quite small-scale units.

The owners' fantasies of vastness had been concentrated on their houses, and some enormous houses had been built. Wentworth Woodhouse covers three acres; Stowe is, and Wanstead was, almost as large. Those still standing house schools or municipal offices or museums, all being too big for private life today. Even by the mid-century the palace 'urge' had lost much of its power: the lives that the rich and noble led were less ceremonial and so had less need for immense and purely ceremonial spaces. Of course, the desire for the display of opulence had by no means abated. It found a different expression. Houses, if new, were seldom vast. Houses were less likely to be completely demolished and rebuilt; they were altered or added to (although Brown himself razed Vanbrugh's Claremont), the new building often mimicking the old. While the largest rooms were now devoted to the display of paintings or sculpture rather than people, the real passion for scale had moved outdoors.

If 'Capability' Brown was called a vandal for demolishing a few ancient and admired houses, they were few indeed compared with the ancient gardens that vanished almost as soon as he looked at them. They were replaced by unimpeded space, and replaced ruthlessly. The Georgian Age was extremely aware of taste and fashion, but the energy behind the change seems to have gone beyond either.

Now that gardens were no longer walled and enclosing, or Kentian and passively pictorial with a strongly directed path of exploration, power and wealth could express themselves not by the complexity of the garden image but by pure breadth of domain. Baroque gardens had expressed a similar sort of territorial instinct, but this was now expressed not by immense avenues leading to the horizon but by swelling lawns, glittering lakes and dusky and distant forests. Like the baroque garden, there was no logical reason (except lack of money) why a Brown landscape should ever stop, or even (except boredom) why one place should look any different to another. Now that palaces were felt necessary only for king and Parliament, magnates seemed to feel that breathtaking Arcadian landscapes around their houses were all the more needed. That these landscapes were, in their own way, quite as artificial as their grandfathers' avenues had been, seemed not to matter. Their owners, tranquil, reasonable, still Augustan, could stroll or ride over scythed lawns, through scenery designed to induce exactly that feeling. They could look back at their pale and symmetrical houses or sail on their sheltered lakes confident that the wealthy of no other nation enjoyed such felicity.

The landscape elements that Brown used were, as we have seen, few. Trees were now disposed in a very characteristic manner, and one which was much imitated by lesser men and much ridiculed by his detractors after

The lake at Bowood (above) and Blenheim.

1780. Conservatively, he followed the maxims of early writers, especially Pope, that had been originally formulated for smaller gardens. He concealed the perimeter of whatever piece of ground he was allotted by a belt of trees. This, thickly planted, usually contained a carriage-ride. As the inside edge of the belt was wavy, the ride would at times have seemed set in deep forest; at others, glimpses of lawn, water and the house would have been seen through the trees. The space enclosed inside the belt was variously planted with more wood, sometimes extensive, more often as isolated clumps of twenty or thirty trees. There was also a number of single trees scattered about as 'specimens'. All the trees were disposed with the greatest subtlety, to emphasize a fine contour or to mask a distant prospect until exactly the right moment. Curiously, he was often accused of deforesting the countryside, and yet he planted far more than he destroyed: at Fisherwick alone more than a million trees were planted.

The second element, water, Brown also used in a masterly way. Even his most violent detractor, Uvedale Price, could not help but admire the lake at Blenheim, and there are many equally splendid examples (especially at Holkham, Heveningham, Bowood and Luton Hoo). As few of these lakes were based on natural ones, they were usually the most expensive feature in any landscape design. Dams had to be built, and often there had to be a series of them. They had to be planted or otherwise disguised. The margins of the lake had to be carved into bays and headlands that often bore little relationship to the original topography. Of course, the lakes had to be as large as possible, the far shore blue with distance, and the near one with green lawns sweeping down to the water's edge, around each clump and grove of new saplings, and directly up to the walls and windows of the house itself. Boundaries and fences could not exist in this spacious and serene world; where there was no ha-ha, curious cattle could (and did) gaze in at the windows of the drawing-room and library.

While Brown landscaped the grounds of many houses that were already ancient, he was also called upon to act as an architect. This gave him the opportunity not only to evolve an integrated landscape but to integrate the house as well. The Palladian ideal of the country house, with its main public rooms on the first floor and its deep portico, and with stables, kitchens and outbuildings attached to the main house as flanking pavilions, no longer impressed new patrons. The approach to the classical idiom became more relaxed and was soon to be no longer the only language of architecture. Brown used a variety of indigenous styles, often with felicity. His houses were never admired for their architectural perfection, judged, as they were, purely as façades: they were admired for their comfort and the convenience of their internal planning. Nevertheless, Brown's new emphasis on three-dimensional landscape was such that the house had to be seen from all sides. This had been much less the case in Palladian houses where the greatest emphasis had been placed on the entrance front, and sometimes a lesser one on the garden front, although not all houses designed by Palladio himself had had wings and pavilions, and even a few neo-Palladian houses in England had been designed 'all round'. This new idea of circulation in space meant that the house's outbuildings cluttered up the hoped-for simplicity and elegance. Stables, coach-houses, lodgings, kitchen and flower gardens, even in some cases the kitchens themselves, were cut away from the house and concealed behind shrubs and clumps of trees. The main house, immaculate, de-odorized, remote from noise, nuisance and chaos was left, to use Walpole's phrase, "grazing by itself in the middle of its park".

An example much visited in the eighteenth century was the already noted Fisherwick. The garden had been designed for the Marquis of Donegal, and was visited by William Marshall in 1784. It was entirely in the Brown manner, having been made out of a flat site, now with artificial hills and valleys, a series of lakes with noisy waterfalls in between, groups of trees, a belt and the older ha-ha disguised by irregular pieces of shrubbery. The house (also by Brown) was seen half a mile distant on entering the park, which Marshall felt lost the effect of surprise, adding that the house, though large, looked insignificant at that distance. He was critical, too, of some of the planting, but admired the "superiorly elegant groves of plane and American firs". Yet of the whole scheme he says that

> forseeing the charming effect which lofty groves, such as the present plantations will probably become a century hence, embracing the house will certainly have, we admit the propriety of the design. . . . His great aim has obviously been to throw the whole place, as seen from the approach, into one grand composition, and has succeeded. . . . The house, too, stately and new, embosomed in aspiring groves and backed by some fine old trees that rise above them, contributes not a little to make up an assemblage which gives the eye and mind great satisfaction.

Fisherwick has not survived. Others have. In all of them, the Arcadian ideal has been carried almost into the realms of abstraction. Most such regions prove ambiguous places.

The real world was far from tranquil. The Stuart cause had been finally destroyed only a few years before 1750, and although for some years Britain was without a foreign war on her hands, there were difficulties on the Continent and grave social problems at home. The economic pace, stimulated by trade and conquest, was quickening. The countryside was becoming enclosed, at last more profitable (many farmhouses and manors date from this period, often replacements of earlier buildings), and the agricultural population was declining. People flocked to the cities, and until the 1780s there were insufficient factories to absorb the extra manpower. Poverty and overcrowding were rife, and with this grew a sense of political grievance, as well as a mania for gin, curbed only by the licensing laws of 1757. Struggles for power at Court, for work and liberty among the populace and for money among those who could make it (even then, social commentators thought that standards of British manufacture were becoming alarmingly poor) must have made, for those who could afford it, an Arcadian garden by Brown a singularly attractive place.

Brown in many ways exemplified the successful self-made man of the period. At the beginning a humble worker in the kitchen gardens of Stowe; he became head gardener, working with William Kent on the improvements to that estate. Soon, having worked for Lords Grafton and Brooke, he set himself up in business. By the end of his career he had been Surveyor to His Majesty's Gardens and Waters, with a house at Hampton Court, had bought an estate at Fenstanton for £13,000, and had married one of his children well. While it was natural for a landscape gardener to want to buy land of his own, this was also the natural response of any man successful in commerce or politics. Those fortunate enough to do so, followed the taste set by the Whig noblemen and employed Brown to do their gardens. By the late 1770s William Mason, in his long and rather dull poem *The English Garden* could mock the earlier style of Kent:

> . . . that Albion's listening youths
> Informed erewhile to scorn the long drawn lines
> Of straight formality, alike may scorn
> Those quick, acute, perplexed and tangled paths
> That, like the snake crushed by the sharpened spade,
> Writhe in convulsive torture, and full oft,
> Through many a dank and unsunned labyrinth,
> Mislead our steps; till giddy, spent and soiled
> We reach the point where first our race began.

But 'Capability' Brown, while creating great beauties, was responsible for the near-death of certain aspects of gardening. He was also responsible for a greatly heightened awareness of landscape itself, something that was to have immense and lasting importance. He established for a while a Poussinesque landscape, but the elements he suppressed became, by the end of the century, once more the rage. They became the rage amid such a welter of philosophizing about garden aesthetics that no one has had the temerity to discuss gardening in the language of the fine arts ever since.

These later shifts in taste, and indeed the social changes that lay beneath them, were scarcely important during Brown's lifetime. Their beginnings lay in two aesthetic movements which, though both primarily architectural, had a considerable effect on gardening, not solely on the buildings in gardens. The two movements were, respectively, the Gothic and the Chinese.

5. The Gothic

In 1750, at a rather small house set in only fourteen acres of ground and once a tenement where the actor Colly Cibber had lodged, the first step had been taken towards the destruction of the new garden style that was only twenty years old. Although that step had, as yet, nothing to do with gardening, within fifty years Arcadia was dead. The step was an architectural one. Horace Walpole had decided that his villa, Strawberry Hill, was to be in the gothic style. This did not immediately lead to the re-creation of gothic gardens (there was none until after the turn of the century), but the sequence of ideas that began at Strawberry Hill soon had a profound effect on landscape and garden design.

Of course, there had been a number of earlier essays in the gothic idiom. Inigo Jones had used 'toy fort' gothic buildings in some of his theatre designs. Vanbrugh used the same style for the garden outworks at Castle Howard and for his own 'castle' at Greenwich. Kent had used it for making sympathetic additions to older buildings. Inveraray Castle, a very large toy fort indeed, also pre-dated Strawberry Hill. Walpole's house was, I think, rather different in intention to these earlier examples. They were fairly amusing essays in a rationalized castle style: Strawberry Hill (based more on ecclesiastical than military architecture) was an attempt to produce a much darker and more emotional response. This did not always succeed, sometimes seeming merely frivolous.

Walpole's public explanation of his decision was based, fairly enough, on an appeal to patriotism: Britain had a perfectly satisfactory indigenous style of building, and there was no need to import one from either Athens, Rome or Peking. In the 1750s there was little critical appreciation of this pre-classical British architecture, and the word 'gothic' was rather vaguely used to cover anything built between the Norman invasion and the death of Elizabeth I. Walpole also pointed out the absurdities of the classical style, the uselessness of deep porticoes or small windows in the windy, wet and cool climate of Britain. By showing these illogicalities, he reduced classicism

Horace Walpole's Strawberry Hill, a gothic house in a conventional landscape; but the interest in Gothicism heralded the end of the landscape garden.

The gothic cottage at Stourhead (Wiltshire).

to a style with no more moral weight than any other, even 'chinoiserie'. He did not, however, point out the similar absurdity of using plaster copies of royal tombs as chimney-pieces, or of wooden battlements on a suburban villa. Nevertheless, the use of the gothic idiom did free architecture (for the first time in a hundred years) from the constraints of symmetry and the necessity of proportion. Strawberry Hill, too, must have been the first house for at least a hundred years to have grown organically, with new rooms and towers added as Walpole needed, or could afford, them. Certainly, this was a complete antithesis to his father's immense, totally symmetrical and rather ponderous house at Houghton, designed and built as a completely unified entity. However superficial Horace Walpole's use of gothic ornament may now seem (especially in the light of the heavily correct gothic architecture of the succeeding century), it was certainly related to the curious fantasies of his novel *The Castle of Otranto*, published in 1765. These showed a desire for physical and emotional excess foreign to the then current emphasis on balance and reason.

However, the gothic idea, whether as architecture or on the page, became increasingly popular. It offered a spicy alternative to the coolness of the classical fashion, allowing some outlet to the often strong side of human nature that revels in disorder, chaos and darkness. While the stories of most gothic novels took place in a strange country composed entirely of landscapes from Salvator Rosa and buildings from Piranesi, it is difficult to feel such excitement at Strawberry Hill. However, for people happy to have their emotions deeply stirred by an obelisk or an urn in the sort of Kentian garden that Brown was to reform, a battlemented turret or an even moderately gloomy cloister, however flimsily built, was enough to produce the whole gothic *frisson* of violence and nightmare. It was only in the next century, with the Romantic movement in full flood, that people allowed their personalities or their houses to become gothic in any sense that would impress the present age.

The new interest in indigenous building styles encouraged many people to begin looking at the old buildings of town and countryside, to understand their qualities and, by the 1770s, to find them beautiful. They were admired for the informality of living that their often unplanned interiors allowed. Many people, building new houses for themselves, tried to copy this pleasantness. However, the most obvious quality of these ancient buildings, especially to the visually uneducated, was simply their age. Ancient houses were set in ancient estates and belonged to ancient families. Few people like to think of themselves as *nouveau riche*; fewer still like others to think them so. By the third quarter of the eighteenth century, with the beginnings of the Industrial Revolution at hand and most sections of the economy booming, there was a great deal of new wealth created. Much of this was in the hands of people who had not previously been rich. Few of them felt secure until they owned land, either socially secure or financially secure. When they were lucky enough to have found an estate, especially one with too small a house, they were faced with the problem of which style to adopt for a new one. Few wanted to emulate the Whig aristocrats in their icy Roman palaces. It was easier, and cheaper, to ape the wealthier gentry. To try to give the shiny newness of their wealth some semblance of age, a house in the gothic style, however spurious, had the right associations, even if it caused to smile the owners of genuinely ancient names and houses (smiles perhaps of avarice, not of condescension).

Before discussing Walpole's own garden, or the influence of the gothic idiom on gardening more generally, it is worth examining an intermediate stage between house and garden. Freed from the functional necessity of providing useful accommodation, garden houses and follies could express mere fashion in the most uninhibited way. It was with them that gothic architecture had its widest influence (even classical houses had gothic pavilions) and the most long lasting (they were still being built at the end of the nineteenth century). The earliest gothic garden building slightly pre-dates Strawberry Hill and was built by Sanderson Miller near his own Radway Grange. He eventually produced quite a number, some even winning Walpole's approval. Most were meant to be ruined castles, but few were particularly sinister. Indeed, few gothic pavilions were. Perhaps they made exciting places in which to read a gothic romance of passion and cruelty (often involving innocent and pretty virgins who were not always saved on the last page). While reading of terrible happenings on cliffs or in caverns, or in the vaults of ruined monasteries perched on immense crags with raging torrents below, the reader could still see beyond the windows (if the glass were not too deeply stained) gently rolling lawns. Somewhere, the cooks were preparing dinner, and maids putting coals on the fire.

Walpole, when asked why his Twickenham garden was not gothic, said that he felt it should be *riant* and gay. As he went on to poke fun at melancholy gardens, he clearly thought of gothic gardens as gloomy, rather than merely formal. His own used the full classical idiom and had nothing to do with medieval England. With its serpentine woods filled with quickly curving paths (he felt that they gave an increased feeling of scale to his ground), with its beds filled with flowering shrubs and herbaceous plants, as well as its lawns and views of the Thames, it must have been as charming as he believed it. Certainly, many prints of it were produced, and one shows the only formal element that it contained; a circular pool set in a beautifully planted enclosure. Incidentally, Walpole was so unashamed of theatrical effect that he even grazed sheep of a particularly small breed on his distant lawns, to enhance the laws of perspective. Details of the garden planting will be dealt with later, but he gardened for many years, and over that time his ideas gradually changed. When he wrote the celebrated *History of the*

Drawings of Sanderson Miller's gothic folly at Wimpole Hall.

Modern Taste in Gardening (in its final form by 1782 although it had been started some years before), he had come to feel that the landscape movement had gone too far. So many of the earlier gardens had vanished that he thought with regret of felled avenues and smoothed-out terraces. It was only ten years later that the first major apologia for formalism was published.

Whatever one may think of Walpole's gothic tendencies, he was eminently sensible about gardening. He saw no reason why the garden in the immediate environs of the house should not be well kept up and as decorative as need be (his comment on taking pasture right up to the walls has already been quoted). He saw, too, no reason why urban gardens should not be completely formalized. Fountains, basins and trellis-work were, he felt, the perfect foils to the architectural environment. In all of this he prefigured the work of Repton and, indeed, a large part of the evolution of taste in the late Georgian period. Curiously, he has nothing to say about the most important, and indeed most bitter, debate of that period: that of the 'Picturesque' and the 'Sublime'. Brought into prominence by the publication of Edmund Burke's *Philosophical Enquiry into the Origin of our Ideas of the Sublime and Beautiful* in 1757, it absorbed much of the emotions and energies that activated the gothic. He seems not to have been interested in the philosophy of aesthetics; he was perhaps more disturbed by the presence of a fashion more directly the foe of gothicism, and to which the derivation of the new landscape style had been attributed. Naturally, the belief that this style had had nothing to do with England was most firmly elaborated by the owners of the style that the new one had supplanted: the French. The country which they claimed had seen its birth was the very distant and very unknown China.

Thomas Robins's drawing of a gothic temple in an unknown garden, probably on the Thames at Old Windsor.

6. China

China, distant and mysterious, had fascinated Europe since the sixteenth century. Its wares had been imported in small quantities and had even begun to be copied by Western craftsmen. By the seventeenth century, screens, cabinets, vases, silks and papers had become immensely fashionable and copied even more. As trade with China increased, so did curiosity about the country that produced such exquisite artefacts, and also the desire to house them in settings appropriate to their origin. By the middle of the eighteenth century China was the rage, and any house with any pretension to fashion had at least one room fitted up in the Chinese style; a style that in fact owed far more to London cabinet-makers, upholsterers and plasterers than it did to China. Nevertheless, the owners were pleased enough and in all probability owned at least a few objects that really had travelled from that distant source.

One of the first descriptions in English of Chinese gardens is in Sir William Temple's *Upon the Gardens of Epicurus*, published in 1685, when all English gardens were still formal. "The Chinese", he wrote, "scorn this way of planting . . . their imagination is employed in continuing figures where the beauties shall be great and strike the eye, without any disposition of parts, that shall be commonly or easily observed. . . . The Chinese have a particular word to express this [studied irregularity of beauty], 'sharawadgi'." Temple had no first-hand knowledge of the Orient but may have met more travelled people during his ambassadorship at The Hague. He would certainly have seen Chinese gardens and landscapes splendidly depicted on lacquer screens and on porcelain. His own garden was a copy of a formal garden he had much admired in his youth. The view of it by Jan Kip shows no attempt at 'sharawadgi', although, outside the bounds of the garden proper, it does show an artificial-looking stream winding through a wilderness.

Early in the next century, Lord Burlington had in his library at Chiswick a book of views of new Chinese imperial gardens engraved by an Italian priest, Matteo Ripa, who had been at the Chinese Court in 1713. No doubt William Kent must have perused it. It seems unlikely, though, that Burlington, such a convinced Roman, would have much to do with a style that was already being thought of as frivolous. Nevertheless, Sir William Chambers, of whom more later, reported that Kent designed furniture for what must have been the first Chinese garden pavilion ever built, 'the House of Confucius' at Kew, designed by a fan-painter called Joseph Goupy in 1745.

The fashion developed a philosophical and political backing. Translations of Confucius had appeared at the end of the seventeenth century and had a profound effect on a number of European thinkers, especially Leibniz, who devoted the rest of his life to that familiar hope, cultural exchange between East and West. China was seen, however incorrectly, as an almost ideal State, devoted to reason and justice and ruled by a benign, compassionate and learned despot. This was a convenient set of beliefs and was taken up as much by the flatterers of European despots as by those who yearned for reason and justice. In England, by mid-century, the informal style of gardening already had strong political undertones, and an increasing knowledge of China for a while augmented these. In France, the English style was at once interpreted as an embodiment of China. This naturally reduced the importance of a political and commercial rival in French eyes, although, as a gesture, the style was known as *anglo-chinois*.

Chinese architecture and ideas travelled more readily than Chinese plants. However many Chinese pavilions were built (to Horace Walpole's disgust), no attempts were made to create authentic Chinese gardens. Repton made some additions in that style at Woburn Abbey, but the first good examples date from the 1900s. The first major piece of polemic designed to further the style was Sir William Chambers's *Dissertation on Oriental Gardening* published in May 1772. It is a most strange work, owing far more to the wild imagination of its author than to his genuine and first-hand experience of China. As a youth, he had spent a short time in Canton, before training as an architect. He had sketched some of the buildings and their contents and later published *Designs of Chinese Buildings*. Of course, the drawings it contained bore·very little relationship to the grotesque architecture that fashionable Europe believed to be the essence of Chinese taste. The book was not a success, although he did obtain one important patroness: the garden of Augusta, Dowager Princess of Wales, soon contained many of the most seriously Chinese buildings of the day. The garden was Kew, and Chambers's pagoda still stands, although rather less decorated than it was originally. Walpole hated them all, realizing that chinoiserie was a very able rival to his beloved gothic. Less partial men failed to distinguish between them. Mason mentions both thus:

> Let those who weekly, from the city's smoke
> Crowd to each neighb'ring hamlet, there to hold

Matteo Ripa's illustrations of the Jehol gardens were in Burlington's collection and may have influenced Kent (a selection on this and the following three pages).

Their dusty Sabbath, tip with gold and red
The milk white palisades, that gothic now,
And now Chinese, now neither, and yet both,
Chequer their trim domain. Thy sylvan scenes
Would fade, indignant at the tawdry glare. . . .

Walpole disliked Chambers personally for other reasons. The two men were
in opposite political camps. Further, the dark imagining that Walpole and
his friends associated only with the gothic and romantic movement is found,
quite powerfully, in Chambers's own writings. Walpole may have felt that
this might win for China some of the devotees of the gothic. Chambers
combined ideas of opulence, sensationalism and sublimity in a way that was
several decades ahead of his time, and proposed a sort of garden that was
totally at odds with the deliberate and elegant shams of Strawberry Hill, and
even more so with the sophisticated beauties of a garden by Brown. Of
Brown, Chambers wrote rudely, "that he was a peasant emerge[d] from the
melon ground to commence professor". Of Brown's gardens, he writes, "A
stranger is often at a loss to know whether he be walking in a meadow, or in a
pleasure ground, made and kept at a very considerable expense." He goes on
to describe a typical layout, and ends with, "And thousands of venerable
plants, whole woods of them, have been swept away to make room for a little
grass and a few American weeds."

Before he embarks on some of his more imaginative descriptions of
Chinese gardens, he does describe some scenes that, but for their alleged
Chinese context, sound as if either Kent or Repton had gardened in Canton.
"Their regular buildings they generally surround with artificial terraces,
slopes and many flights of steps; the angles of which are adorned with
groups of sculpture and vases", and, he goes on (and this does seem like a
backward look at Kent and his followers), they put "inscriptions, verses and
moral sentiments" all round the garden to characterize and distinguish the
different scenes. Of gardens generally, "the usual method . . . is to contrive a
great variety of scenes, to be seen from certain points of view; at which are
placed seats or buildings, adapted to the different purposes of mental or
sensual enjoyment." Of the latter, he gives a remarkable description of
Chinese 'Gardens of Love' which would have considerably enlivened the
English countryside had they been adopted there. These opulent wildernesses
were filled with flowers, rare fowl, statues, grottoes and pavilions inhabited
by a myriad seducers. He also describes some architecturally remarkable
pavilions, some built of roots and pollards (these were taken up and
hundreds appeared in British gardens well into the nineteenth century), and
also "'Halls of the Moon', of a prodigious size; composed each of one
single vaulted room, made in the shape of a hemisphere; the concave of which
. . . pierced with an infinite number of little windows, made to represent the
moon and stars." Such a building, or rather a design for it, forms almost the

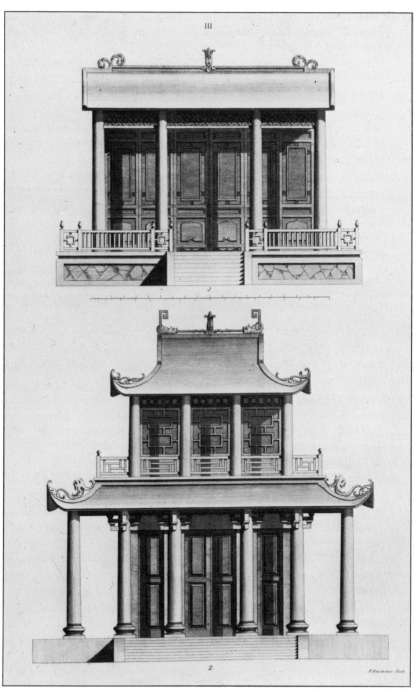

William Chambers's 'Designs of Chinese buildings' of 1757 were the first based on first-hand knowledge and were in contrast to his suggestions for the surrounding gardens.

peak of the whole neo-classical movement, to be described later. The drawings, of a cenotaph for Sir Isaac Newton, by Boulée, are dated 1784. Perhaps they derive from Sir William Chambers.

Chambers was plainly no botanist. His knowledge of the Chinese flora is non-existent; his descriptions of planting in Chinese gardens makes exclusive use of plants commonly to be seen in those of Britain. They are now no less interesting for that, and are quoted in a later chapter. Of Chambers's imagination, of its affinity with gothic and of its importance in the later development of the English landscape style, the following passage is relevant:

> Their scenes of terror are composed of gloomy woods, deep valleys inaccessible to the sun, impending barren rock, dark caverns and impetuous cataracts rushing down the mountains from all parts. The trees are ill-formed, forced out of their natural direction and seemingly torn to pieces by the violence of tempests . . . the buildings are in ruins, or half consumed by fire . . . gibbets, crosses, wheels and the whole apparatus of torture are seen from the roads . . . and to add to both the horror and the sublimity of these scenes, they sometimes conceal in cavities, on the summits of the highest mountains, foundries, lime kilns and glass works; which send forth large volumes of flame. . . .

England, not China, had factories of such scale, and even they only became objects of sublime meditation two or three decades later. After describing gardens of the supernatural, with images of dead kings and water-powered flutes and organs to provide background music, he progresses

> through dark passages cut through the rocks, on the sides of which are . . . colossal dragons, infernal fiends and other horrid forms, which hold in their monstrous talons . . . preparations that yield a constant flame, serving at once to guide and astonish the passenger; from time to time he is surprised with repeated shocks of electrical impulse, with showers of artificial rain . . . instantaneous explosions of fire . . . many different sounds, some resembling the cries of men in torture . . . howls of ferocious animals. . . .

And so he goes on; all rather more exciting that a walk around the lake at Stourhead or a stroll at Claremont. Patrick Neill, a Scotsman who visited a number of continental *jardins anglo-chinois* in 1816, was much put out by being fooled by some stone sheep in a field; his response to the sort of garden propounded by Chambers may be imagined.

It is perhaps unfair to Chambers to emphasize the wildness of his schemes. Later, he gives a clear criticism of some of the faults of the current garden style:

> Neither do they [the Chinese] ever carry a walk round the extremities of a piece of ground, and leave the middle entirely open, as is too often done amongst us; for though it might render the first glance striking and noble, they think the pleasure would be of short duration, and that the spectator would be but

moderately entertained, by walking several miles with the same objects continually obtruding upon his sight. . . . In their crooked walks they carefully avoid all sudden or unnatural windings, particularly the regular serpentine curves of which our English gardeners are so fond; observing that these eternal, uniform, undulating lines are, of all things, the most unnatural, the most affected and the most tiresome to pursue. Having nature in view, they seldom turn their walks without some apparent excuse. . . .

That is Chambers's main criticism; that the Brownian garden was, above all, artificial, that it was more truly natural to allow a garden to exhibit its artificiality (however expressed) and let nature have its own way beyond the bounds. That part of Chambers's message was enthusiastically taken up in the following decades.

Chambers himself rejected chinoiserie later in his career, believing finally that the classical idiom was the only valid means of expression. Elsewhere, the whole Chinese fantasy slowly died away, except for a few late-Georgian pagodas (for example, at Alton Towers) and the Chinese Dairy at Woburn, set among genuinely Chinese plants. It was the increasing familiarity with the real China (new plants, too, began to flood in) that disposed of the hoped-for China of fantasy. By 1827 a visitor to Canton found the gardens "ridiculously fantastic", with weird layouts and even positively dangerous (he was referring to rickety bridges, not anything more spectacular). If knowledge provided a cure for chinoiserie, gothicism, being a cult of the past, had no similar antidote and retained a formidable power for another hundred years.

Thomas Robins's painting shows the insubstantial, if charming, nature of much *chinoiserie* garden ornament.

7. Beauty and function

Throughout the second half of the eighteenth century, indeed until the Romantic movement swept all before it in the reign of George IV, no one doubted the very real existence of an external and universally recognizable quality called 'Beauty'. This beauty, not yet being in the eye of the beholder (that was part of the Romantic), was something to be seen only by the educated eye (and was second nature to the aristocratic one). The ability to see it was called 'taste', and taste was absolutely essential to social advancement and arrival. Only artists occupied an ambiguous position in this arrangement.

In gardening, the ancient rich had no problems: their houses were built, and their vast acres, even if not yet modified by Kent or Brown, showed at least their venerable age. The new rich, as we have seen, faced a number of frightening decisions. While there were slender intellectual arguments put forward for the various styles of building and gardening, none was powerful enough to place decisively one style ahead of the others. The belief in ranking (and rank) was universal; everyone felt that only one style could be the correct one (usually their own) and that all the others must be wrong and therefore show 'bad' taste. There were no alternative equals. To have bad taste was a far graver solecism than rapacity, corruptness or sexual depravity. Proponents of one style attacked all others with a corresponding degree of intensity and ingenuity. However, for the owner of a small estate there was one remarkable way in which the difficult choice could be avoided, and one which was to be of the greatest importance not only to garden design but also to the awareness of nature and society. This style of gardening was to create on one's land a *ferme orneé*.

As we have seen in Chapter 1, Stephen Switzer had suggested the idea of combining farm and garden. Addison had published a similar suggestion rather earlier, in an issue of the *Spectator* for 1712. In this, he said:

> But why may not the whole be thrown into a kind of garden by frequent plantations, that may turn as much to the profit as the pleasure of the owner....

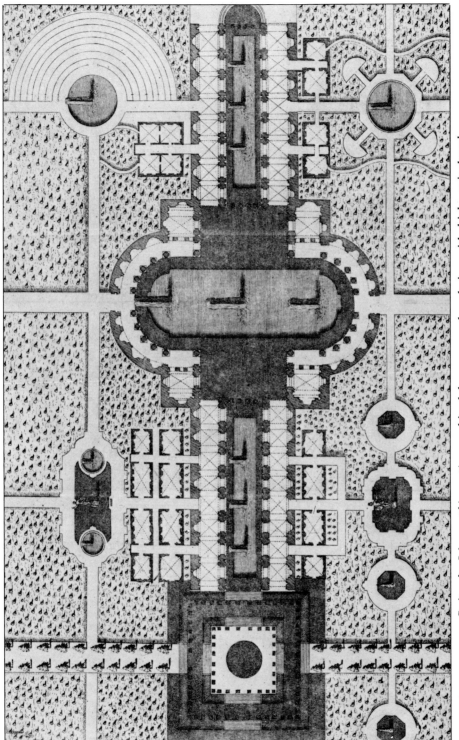

Switzer's *Ichnographia rustica* combined baroque garden design with high agricultural productivity.

> Fields of corn make a pleasant prospect, and if the walks were a little taken care of that lie between them, if the natural embroidery of the meadows were helped and improved by some small additions of art, and the several rows of hedges set off by trees and flowers that the soil was capable of receiving, a man might make a pretty landscape of his own possessions. . . .

It seems unlikely that he went quite so far himself, his estate in Warwickshire still retaining many entirely formal elements. However, he did later go on to say: "I have several acres about my house, and which a skilful gardener would not know what to call. It is a confusion of kitchen garden and parterre, orchard and flower garden, which lie so mixed and interwoven with one another. . . ." Switzer's ideas were at least partly developed from this source, although some of his projected schemes were quite grandiose and designed throughout in a fully baroque way. Fifty years later, this was by no means the effect required. The intention of a *ferme ornée* was to take a piece of farmland and prettify it so that most of it could offer at least some visual delight. Unimproved farmland was not yet found to be beautiful, perhaps because it was itself too new a phenomenon (enclosure of land was still unfinished by the end of the century) to be really appreciated. The 'landscape' we see now, and so often admire, was then young, with a few spindly hedgerows and a few mature trees.

Newly enclosed, or semi-mature enclosed, land could be decorated in a number of ways. The most usual was to substitute, where possible, ornamental and exotic tree and hedge species for the more familiar natives. Hedgerows were draped with jasmine and roses; muddy tracks became trim walks of sand or gravel (Switzer had suggested cockleshells) for the ladies of the house; untidy lanes, cleared and suitably planted, became carriage-rides. Ugly buildings were prettified, disguised as ruins or towers, or demolished. Ugly functions were ignored. It all had powerful attractions. Why shouldn't a functional landscape be decorative? Why shouldn't a garden provide some, at least, of its owner's income? The only danger, apart from poisoning the cattle with exotic vegetation, was that of submerging the hard and often unpleasant drudgery of farming beneath a tide of unsuitable sentiment.

J. C. Loudon ranks the *ferme ornée* only beneath the villa (a term then used of more substantial houses than it is today):

> The *ferme ornée* differs from a common farm in having a better dwelling-house, neater approach, and one partly or entirely distinct from that which leads to the offices. It also differs as to hedges, which are allowed to grow wild and irregular and are bordered on each side by a broad green drive and sometimes by a gravel-walk and shrubs. It differs from a villa in having no park. A dry hilly soil is best suited to this description of residence, and there are some fine examples in Surrey, Kent and the Isle of Wight.

By the time Loudon wrote that description, the *ferme ornée* had begun to look very little like the two most famous and influential exemplars. Indeed,

Shenstone's home, 'The Leasowes', where Art triumphed over Agriculture and the owner lived in poverty.

Woburn Farm: Philip Southcote's much-admired *ferme ornée* was arcadian but still moderately productive.

the one in Surrey had already lost its original character. This was Woburn (or Woodburn) Farm owned and designed by Philip Southcote, and begun in the 1730s. The house shown in contemporary prints is in fact several degrees better than a farmhouse, although the land dependent on it amounted to only one hundred and fifty acres. It was on a flat site, although with a river, and while thirty-five acres were devoted to a conventional garden, the fields were profusely strewn with groves of trees and flowerbeds (fenced presumably, for the farm produced a reasonable amount of cattle) and the hedges suitably intertwined. The trees were exclusively exotic and were as much admired as the whole farm, although Whately (a very influential writer, if somewhat strait-laced) found it "licentious". Even the more flamboyant Horace Walpole felt that "the profusion of flowers and the delicacy of keeping betray more wealthy expense than is consistent with the economy of a farmer or the rusticity of labour. Woburn Farm . . . is the habitation of such nymphs and shepherds as are represented in landscapes and novels, but do not exist in nature. . . ."

The second very important example was The Leasowes, a small estate owned by the poet William Shenstone, near Halesowen in Shropshire. Agricultural productivity was less important here than at Woburn, sadly so, and it became very much the canvas upon which Shenstone could paint his own particular Arcadian fantasies. Several of William Marshall's disparaging comments on it have already been quoted, but one more is worth giving; "What has farming to do with temples, statues, vases, mottoes, mock priories and artificial cascades? Yet do away with these, and who would visit The Leasowes?" He goes on to make a plea for neat and pretty, but natural, farms and points out that "had poor Shenstone adopted this idea, he might yet have lived to enjoy his place; or while he had lived, might have been happy. It was the expensive baubles we have seen, which threw him on the rack of poverty. . . ." Shenstone no doubt preferred influence and acquaintance with the aristocracy to comfort. He advised on the design of a number of gardens, but never in a professional capacity. His garden, despite its fame, began to decay soon after his death. There was little left in the nineteenth century, and now most is beneath suburban houses.

Whatever one may feel about the worst sorts of *ferme ornée* and the sentimentalism to which they gave rise (the most extraordinary example of all being the bizarre one in the park of the Petit Trianon, built for Marie Antoinette in the early 1780s), they gave rise to some important developments. Before a natural farm could be decorated, it first had to be seen. The pattern of the hedgerows on the hillside had to be studied. The banks of the lanes had to be carefully examined to see where planting would be most effective. Nature was examined more widely than it had ever been before. Furthermore, agricultural processes themselves were examined, and ideas of agricultural and visual improvement became closely associated.

Some of the very largest estates became virtually *fermes ornées*, with Holkham and Shugborough as leading examples. Both estates showed another important development. With the new examination of farming, the housing of estate workers and of farm animals was also looked at in a new way. On small estates, this was necessary because such elements had to be brought into the over-all picture of the landscape; they were too close to the main house to ignore. On large estates, this was perhaps less important, but it was soon realized that a comfortable and well-housed workforce worked well, and well-housed beasts were more profitable. At Holkham, the village houses were all rebuilt from 1789; at Shugborough, the great mid-century landscape garden was put to farming from 1795, with splendid buildings by Wyatt; the famous village of Blaise was built, by Nash, from 1810. There are many other examples, although it should be remembered that they are outnumbered by the villages demolished in the earlier part of the century to make way for the landscape. Further, from the beginning of the nineteenth century, architects (hopeful and established) brought out dozens of books of designs for cottages that would look well from the drawing-room windows. If the owners of ornamented farms made some of the biggest improvements in agricultural conditions, it was partly at the moral cost of making the labourer and his family part of the decoration.

The geographical distribution of late-Georgian *fermes ornées* was not, as Loudon thought, a matter of the favourable geology about London. It was the widespread prosperity of the rapidly expanding professional class in that city, and to a lesser extent in all major towns. This wealth needed an outlet into land, while the owners' main source of income remained in the city. However, while the growth of the middle class was soon to have a profound effect on garden design and had already, through the medium of the *ferme ornée*, allowed an appreciation of the artificial landscapes of agriculture, other changes were also taking place that allowed the appreciation of unimproved (and indeed, unimprovable) landscape. This appreciation, a development of part of the gothic idea, was concerned with far grander issues than the combination of charm and profit; the concern was with a much deeper analysis of the nature of beauty and, further, with the pursuit of the 'Sublime'.

8. Cracks in Arcadia

By 1800 Arcadia was clearly dying. There were many causes, as is common in old age, even of a fashion. Some, already discussed, were to do with the nature of taste itself. Others were associated with two revolutions.

Although the beginning of the Industrial Revolution has been dated to a wide range of years, most economic historians agree that it was in full spate by the late 1780s and that it continued to gather momentum for the rest of the period. Leading sectors were cotton and iron, with major associated investments such as canal-building and road-making. The banking system was growing to keep pace (there were twelve country banks in 1750, seven hundred by 1815); exporters were finding immense markets, especially in the Americas, which by 1800 absorbed almost 40 per cent of all exports. For only the most inept or the most unlucky entrepreneurs did any of this mean lost money. The population of the country was rising by about 8 per cent per decade from 1760 to 1800, many souls vanishing into the new large-scale factories, loud, noisy, billowing with steam from new steam-engines (none being integrated into the wilder sort of 'Chinese' landscape). The interest of the country as a whole, and with it that of the artist, designer and man of taste, was turning from the countryside to the town. Urban design, urban landscape, became widely important for the first time, at least for the urban middle and professional classes – classes becoming increasingly powerful economically and politically.

Abroad, the French Revolution was causing political and military turmoil until 1815 (and was associated with rapid changes in taste for those interested in such things who managed to survive). In England, it caused considerable worry to rich men who were not under immediate threat of bloodshed. Many believed it quite likely that the guillotine would follow the major French exports of the period: ideas of liberty, equality and fraternity. Many landed gentlemen began to learn trades and professions, so that if their estates were lost or their stocks became valueless, but they kept their lives, they would at least have bread. Others bought transportable gold or gems. Yet others simply spent more heavily.

Although some new Arcadias were created (even the amazing Fonthill was a remaking of an already splendid mid-century garden), there was never again the feeling that they were permanent. Too many in France lay pillaged and overgrown. For the rest of the period, unease keeps showing in the gardening works published. Almost all of them saw 'horticulture' as a means of stabilizing the political aspirations of both agricultural and urban proletariat. Loudon equates a just society with one where the ownership of land is widely spread, and where landscape gardening would be impossible. He says that the inheritance of property enhances design, as people are willing to plant for a future they will not see.

> But partial rights of this sort are much more injurious than beneficial to society, by giving the privileged party a legal title to contract debts which he is not able to pay. They are remains of those feudal or primitive institutions which, as mankind becomes enlightened, will be swept away, with various other antiquated customs and absurdities, till man at last, whatever may be the circumstances of fortune or family under which he may have been ushered into society, will be left to rise or sink in wealth and respect, according to his personal merits.

Johnson's *History of English Gardening* (1822) has this to say of labourers' gardens: "When the lower order of a state are contented, the abettors of anarchy cabal for the destruction of its civil tranquillity in vain, for they have to efface the strongest of all earthly associations, home and its hallowed accompaniments, for the attachment of the labourer, before he will assist in tearing them from others, in the struggle to effect which, he has nothing definite to gain, and all those flowers of life to lose." Even Uvedale Price (who will figure largely in the next chapter), tolerant of almost all men except 'Capability' Brown, says, "were they [the allowances that some landowners made to all who wished to walk in and enjoy their estates] general throughout the kingdom, they would do much more towards guarding us against democratical opinions."

Abroad, our Arcadias were viewed with alarm. The *Gardeners' Magazine* of 1826 reported a gentleman, writing in a Prussian equivalent, as being amazed at the wealth of our aristocracy. Of Eaton Hall, he said: "At last, we discover through a mass of dark wood, the house itself, in a style of splendour and grandeur truly royal, and such as one would feel almost inclined to call too arrogant for a private individual." He was particularly shocked at the parks of Blenheim, Woburn and Ashridge and the "arrogance, extravagance, and egotism" of the English, which he "would be sorry to see imitated in Germany, further than in a very slight degree".

One result of Britain's rapidly expanding export network was that new areas were constantly being opened up for exploration, not only by traders but also by botanists. In the reign of George I, only 182 new species were

Immense numbers of topographical prints were produced to satisfy an increasing interest in the wilder aspects of the natural landscape. *Above:* Buttermere Water. *Below:* 'Winandermere Lake' (Lake Windermere). *Right:* The upper cascade, Rydale.

introduced to gardening. In that of George II, the number was 1,770. In the following reign, it was 6,056. However, after 1800, more than 150 species were being introduced each year. Everyone interested in gardening was anxious to grow as many of these new wonders as possible, but it was soon found to be impossible to integrate them into the established framework of the idyllic and classical gardens of twenty or thirty years before. Exotic colours and forms would clash. Many gardeners adopted the obvious plan of grouping plants from particular countries together (American gardens will be described later, as will the much rarer attempts at Oriental ones), but there were no aesthetic principles available from English landscape designers on how this was to be done. With so much potential, sleek green lawns, with clumps and belts of largely native trees, suddenly seemed terribly tame and boring.

It was not only foreign climes and foreign plants that were the goal of the explorer. Vast tracts of Great Britain herself were virtually unknown to the southern rich, or even the landowners and gardeners of Yorkshire or the Scottish Borders. The Lake District, the Scottish Highlands, the Welsh mountains, had all been deemed drear and horrid earlier in the eighteenth century, certainly not places to visit for pleasure or instruction. Although some travel journals to these areas date from the 1770s (and had been very successful), fifty years later the Highlands and the Lakes, if not yet overrun, were becoming popular places for the adventurous. The lives led by the inhabitants proved to be often quite as exotic as those from far more distant regions and were the subject of excited interest. Now the general interest in landscape and nature that had been the impetus behind the origins of the 'landscape' garden movement had expanded far beyond the confines of either garden or estate, it was small wonder that the traveller's garden (or that of his reader) seemed lacking in drama, wildness and space.

With the expansion of 'landscape' beyond the garden hedge, a shift in the relationship between house and garden became possible. During the mid-century years each had been seen as a setting for the other, almost as self-sufficient symbols of the wealth, taste and breeding of the owner, and which existed almost independently of him. In the 1790s gardens began to be designed not sculpturally but as a view to be seen from inside the house, and so contributing materially to the pleasures of the occupants. In the following ten years houses, too, began to be designed exclusively for comfort and convenience. Kitchen gardens, stables, conservatories, were all moved back and attached to the main residence. (The architectural means of uniting all these elements, and integrating them with the garden, is described in the next chapter.)

The 'view from the window' movement gave rise to some slight absurdities. Even the generally sensible William Marshall writes: "The improvements, and the rooms from which they are to be seen, should be in *unison.* Thus, the view from the drawing-room should be highly embellished, to correspond with the beauty and elegance within. . . . The breakfasting room should have more masculine objects in view and an extended country from the eye to roam over, such as allures us, imperceptibly, to the ride or the chase. The eating and banqueting rooms need no *exterior* allurement." A nice idea, but probably difficult to realize in practise without a very odd-shaped house indeed.

By the last decades of the eighteenth century several strands of thought had coalesced into a strong and counter-revolutionary nostalgia for old formal gardens. Walpole, in the *History* of 1780, began to feel that

> In some lights the reformation seems to have been pushed too far. Though an avenue . . . intercepting views from the seat to which it leads, are capital faults, yet a great avenue . . . has a noble air and . . . announces the habitation of some man of distinction. In other places the banishment of all particular neatness about a house, which is frequently left grazing by itself in the middle of a park, is a defect. Sheltered and even close walks in so very uncertain a climate as ours, are comforts ill exchanged for the few picturesque days that we enjoy: and whenever a family can purloin a warm and even something of an old-fashioned garden from the landscape designed for them by the undertaker in fashion . . . they will find satisfaction on those days that do not invite strangers to come and see their improvements.

Three years later, and under a very similar title, is William Falconer's *Historical view of the Taste for Gardening*. Although not advocating an immediate return to formalism, the author clearly shows that almost every element in the old formal gardens, especially of Italy, was related to the climate in which they originated. Still feeling that Pliny the Younger's taste for topiary was vulgar, even if Pliny "appears at intervals sensible of the superior beauties of unornamented nature", which anyway was common among the later Romans, Falconer goes on to say: "Let us then consider taste not only as general but also as a *relative* principle. To follow nature is to pursue such measures as necessity, the mother of invention, dictates, and although these suggestions [of formality in gardens] may at times be perverted or overstrained, we may be certain that their general tendency is rational, and proper to be attended to."

A last quotation, from Uvedale Price's *Essays on the Picturesque* is the most poignant:

> I may perhaps have spoken more feelingly on this subject from having done myself what I so condemn in others – destroyed an old-fashioned garden. It was not indeed in the high style of those I have described, but it had many circumstances of a similar kind and effect. As I have long since perceived the advantage which I could have made of them, and how much I could have added to that effect, how well I could have in parts mixed the modern style and have altered and concealed many of the stiff and glaring formalities, I have long

77

regretted its destruction. I destroyed it, not from disliking it; on the contrary, it was a sacrifice I made against my own sensations to the prevailing opinion. . . .

He gives a description of its walls, terraces, warm and sheltered walks, statues and splendid iron gateways, and a beautiful summerhouse covered in ancient creepers. He pulled everything down.

My object (as far as I had any determinate object besides that of being in the fashion) was, I imagine, to restore the grounds to what might be supposed its original state; I probably have in some degree succeeded, and after much difficulty, expense and dirt, I have made it look like many other parts of mine and of all beautiful grounds; with but little to mark the difference between what is close to the house and what is at a distance from it; between the habitation of man and that of sheep.

Gainsborough's painting shows the landscape at Foxley after the destruction of the old formal garden.

9. *The new language*

'Capability' Brown died of a heart attack in London on 6 February 1783. Up to the moment of his death he was still at work designing gardens, and died almost as wealthy as some of his patrons. His death created a vacuum at the heart of the landscape design movement that was left unfilled for five years. Although he had both imitators and pupils, none stepped forward to fill his place. Perhaps none had the talent or the force of personality. Probably the most important reason was that many patrons were aware that a major change in taste was imminent and were naturally unwilling to commit themselves to a major expense before they knew what it was to be. It turned out to be a shift from the emotional world of Claude and Poussin to the more dramatic one of Rosa and Dughet.

The shift was accomplished by three main routes. The first, described in the chapters on China and the Gothic, was indebted to Salvator Rosa and became a major part of the Romantic movement. This, with its elevation of intuition over reason and of personal fulfilment over the needs of a hierarchic society, led on to 'the Sublime' (a region where man found himself to be the equal of the gods), and in France led on to Revolution. The second, of which the *ferme ornée* was a part, was compounded of awareness of the natural world, of social awareness and a belief in the superior moral value of the primitive. This, finding a golden age earlier and purer than either the Roman Empire or the Republic, led on to neo-classicism and the Greek Revival. The third (to be briefly described in Chapter 11) was the rapidly increasing number of plants introduced to gardening. This elevated diversity of form and brilliance of colour over the restraint of both in the typical gardens of Brown.

The first two directions were of concern far beyond the confines of the garden, being central to the political and aesthetic issues of the day. Within the garden, although the debate on what should replace Brown's style raged noisily (especially between Humphry Repton, Uvedale Price and Richard Payne Knight), it became curiously divorced from real gardens. Neither

Price nor Knight, both being landed gentlemen, was a practising landscape designer, and so the intellectual programme they represented was never put to the test in any substantial way. Repton designed hundreds of gardens but was not, as we shall see, an intellectual. The third direction, of little concern as yet beyond the garden, was the one that actually triumphed. It was invested with no intellectual content; both Price and Knight accepted it without demur; and Repton designed some marvellous gardens to accommodate it.

'The Sublime' is beyond the scope of this book; it is not possible to create a 'sublime' garden. Mountain peaks, dark canyons and immense plains are the property of the traveller, the writer and the painter (John Martin and de Loutherbourg painted the sublime landscape quite often). However, neo-classicism, a term restricted to architecture, had a gardening parallel. From the middle of the eighteenth century patrons and architects had become aware that there was more to Roman architecture than Palladio and Serlio had allowed. While Venice, Florence and Rome remained crammed with Grand Tourists, more adventurous souls travelled further south, to Naples and beyond. There they discovered the temples at Paestum, first surveyed in 1750, mysterious buildings with columns showing a severe and almost brutal order. While many travellers found them archaic and ugly and returned north, others travelled on to Greece and marvelled at the Athenian Acropolis, now so famous. This was not surveyed until 1762, and the first drawings were made two years later by James Stuart, although not published in England until 1789. The Elgin Marbles arrived in 1802, but by then the Greek Revival was in full swing, and many of its fundamental ideas were beginning to affect gardening.

We have already seen some of the problems set when the classical idiom was challenged by the Gothic and the Chinese. By the beginning of the nineteenth century other styles of building were coming into vogue. Sezincote was Indian; gothic had received an astonishing reinforcement at Fonthill, and an interest in Roman domestic and Italian Renaissance architecture was growing. While such diversity was grist to mill of the Romantic movement, those who had not yet thrown off the Age of Reason still believed that there must be an absolute value somewhere on which to base ideas of taste and beauty. Many patrons decided, logically, that Roman architecture, as it had really been, was 'better', more 'truthful', and therefore more beautiful, than that same architecture seen through the eyes, however perceptive, of sixteenth-century architects. Correctness became an easy substitute for beauty. It also gave rise to a progression: if Roman was better than Palladian, and Roman was known by the Romans to be a corruption of the Greek, then Greek must be even better than Roman. Other justifications were found as well. Many surviving Greek buildings were thought to have been built before Pericles ruled Athens, and so Greek

De Loutherbourg's 'Lake Scene' shows a Sublime landscape that could not be recreated in the garden.

Martin, when being less than Sublime, saw the Garden of Eden as a sub-tropical landscape in the latest fashion.

Doric became associated with republicanism, liberalism and personal freedom (all very romantic). As such it was taken up by the *avant garde*, especially in France where the style was taken to extraordinary lengths of bombast and dehumanization. In England, always less extreme, the first Doric building was a garden pavilion, built at Hagley by James Stuart in 1758.

By the year of Brown's death, such ideas had seeped into the garden. While not immediately manifested in attempts to re-create ancient gardens, a new need was felt for 'truth to Nature' comparable with that quality in Greek Doric and with no pretences to a false Arcadia. A violent attack on such gardens was mounted by Uvedale Price, who seemed to have an obsessive dislike of Brown, which he expressed at great length. "Brown", he said, "was bred a gardener, and having nothing of the mind [he is comparing him with Claude] or eye of a painter, he formed his style, or rather his plan, upon the model of a parterre, and transformed its minute beauties, its little clumps, knots, patches of flowers, the oval belt that surrounds it, and all its twists and crinkim-crankums, to the great scale of Nature." Price saw no difference between the old canal with its straight lines and its angles, and the regularly serpentine streams with edges as naked and uniform as before. This now seems very unfair, but many of Brown's landscapes in the early 1800s will have looked quite different from the mature and shaggy scenes of today, of which Price would probably approve.

Associated with this impatience with the Brownian garden was a loss of interest in 'beauty' itself. Following the publication of Burke's *Philosophical Enquiry into the Origin of our Ideas of the Sublime and Beautiful* in 1757, the notion of beauty was generally held to consist of smooth flowing lines, of smoothness of surface and of clear, bright colours. Beneath the veil of his (and others') attempts at the analysis of beauty can be seen the gentle form of a woman's body. 'The Sublime' was an altogether different quality, nowadays usually described as awe, being the sensuous enjoyment of the magnificently terrible, the vast or even the horrible. Its landscape equivalents have already been mentioned. The arcadias of Lancelot Brown were known to be beautiful, and were certainly so in Burke's sense. It was beautiful, and tame. It was also completely unnatural. As 'the Sublime' was impossible, some intermediate state was required, and this became known as 'the Picturesque'. The word has nowadays no clearly defined meaning, being synonymous with 'quaint' or 'pretty'. It first appeared in William Gilpin's *Dialogue at Stowe* of 1748 and was later much used by him in the series of published journals of tours he made throughout the British Isles from 1770. These were very successful. For him, 'picturesque' beauty was that sort which was most suitably depicted in a picture. Scenes with strong light and shade, trees with bold and striking shapes, and lesser vegetation with spectacular foliage, were all picturesque. Suitable compositions divided neatly into foreground, mid-ground and distance (all this was rarely combined in nature). Almost anything with a rough texture, from a thatched cottage to an ancient donkey, was the object of interest and admiration.

Critics were quick to point out the absurdity of finding a wrinkled crone, a battered horse or a decaying village more exciting than a beautiful girl, a racehorse or a model settlement. When Uvedale Price took up 'the Picturesque', he found the most perfect expression of it not in nature but once again in the landscape paintings of the Italian seventeenth century. He pointed out, correctly, that no painting depicted a lawn or clumps of trees that in any way approached those found in a Brown landscape. The water's edge was never so neat and tidy in either painting or nature. Paintings, themselves artificial, were once again taken as models for nature, and so for 'the Picturesque' garden. The same paintings which had given a language of design to gardens in the 1730s, gave a second and quite different language to it seventy years later. Naturally, it was open to many of the same objections. Because of the needs of composition, Price advocated the use of foregrounds which were, in the painterly tradition, to consist of docks and acanthus, decaying fences, gnarled trees and other bits and pieces. Repton quickly pointed out that continuous foregrounds were an impossibility in a landscape that was meant to be ridden or walked through. He also pointed out that in real life the eye was able to see a much wider angle of vision, vertical as well as horizontal, than any painting could contain. The same rules of composition could not even be applied when the spectator was static. Of course, Repton was on rather shaky ground, for the schemes he presented to possible clients (the famous Red Books) were based on his own watercolours, in which the designs were worked out in an entirely painterly way. Perhaps aware of these difficulties, he vehemently attacked what he called "the wild improvers" for wanting to strew gardens with such rank weeds and ranker rubbish that they would constitute a hazard to the health of any patron foolish enough to countenance it. Price at once published a lengthy denial.

As neither Price nor Knight would condescend to design any ground but his own (and as we have seen, Price was not entirely happy with what he had done), no fully 'picturesque' landscapes were created, although the gardens at Deepdene, Scotney and Belsay approached it. However, many 'picturesque' houses did develop, derived in part from neo-classicism but mainly from the paintings of Caspar Dughet, which were found to contain dwelling-houses (peasant rather than patrician) that splendidly contrived to be both classical and asymmetrical. Real advances in real garden design were left to Humphry Repton, and he had little time for truth to real nature: only the appearance was important. In *Sketches and Hints in Landscape Gardening* of 1794, he wrote

Thomas Hope was his own
designer at Deepdene and
created a rare example of the
Picturesque garden.

... It is the business of taste, in all the polite arts, to avail itself of stratagems by which the imagination may be deceived. . . . The perfection of landscape gardening consists in the four following requisites: First, it must display all natural beauties and hide all natural defects of every situation. Secondly, it should give the appearance of extent and freedom by carefully disguising or hiding the boundary. Thirdly, it must studiously conceal every interference of art, however expensive, by which the scenery is improved; making the whole appear the production of nature only; and, fourthly, all objects of mere convenience or comfort, if incapable of being ornamental, or of becoming proper parts of the general scenery, must be removed or concealed.

Repton was no patrician: his father was a minor Customs official; he himself was a failed businessman and farmer and had decided, in a moment of opportunism, that he should be the new man to follow Brown. He had very few qualifications for this, apart from being a reasonably accomplished watercolourist and having an agreeable social address (which included the lavish use of flattery). His education had been not for scholarship but for business (under the tutelage of the very rich Hope family in Holland, one of whose members will be mentioned later). It may have been his contact with the wider world that gave him such a grasp of the spirit of the age.

Repton's first landscape commissions date from 1788, five years after the death of 'Capability' Brown. Although, during the course of his career, he had a number of very extensive grounds to design, the largest number of his patrons were the new moderately rich, none of whom had large estates. For them he could write: "The first essential of greatness in a place is the appearance of united and uninterrupted property; and it is in vain if this is studied within the pale, if it is only too visibly contradicted without it. . . ." He goes on to suggest that the local church or some other public building should be decorated in the style of the house, or that the local inn should hang the family coat of arms. Failing this, an imposing gateway should be built as near the village or town as possible. Richard Knight at once proposed, ironically, that a map of the estate should be hung up outside the porter's lodge.

Later in his life, Repton found such things less important. In a *Fragment on Hare Street* (the location of his modest house), he says: "I have lived to see many of my plans beautifully realized, but many more cruelly marred; sometimes by false economy, sometimes by injudicious extravagance. I have also reached that period when the improvement of houses and gardens is more delightful to me than that of parks or forests, landscapes or distant prospects." However, he designed some splendid prospects, several of which are now at the peak of their perfection, notably Sheringham and Luscombe Castle.

In spite of all the debate on how grounds should look and whether the house should be Greek, Roman, Italian, Egyptian, Indian or Repton's own rather wishy-washy 'Tudorbethan', there was no debate at all on how the gardens closest to the house should be laid out. There, the three warriors of 'the Picturesque' reached consensus. It was foreshadowed when Walpole wrote in 1768: "They talk of shady groves, purling streams and cooling pinches Chloe's nose 'till it is red and blue. . . . Taste is too freezing a Zephyr is a north-east wind that makes Damon button up his chin, and pinches Chloe's nose 'till it is red and blue. . . .' Taste is too freezing a commodity for us and, depend upon it, will go out of fashion again." He was right. One of the first descriptions of the sort of late-Georgian garden that replaced the 'shady groves' was published in defence of Repton by one of his early patrons;

> I hope therefore, that you will pursue the system that I conceive you to have adopted, and vindicate to the art of laying out ground its true principles, which are wholly different from those which the wild improvers would wish to introduce. Places are not to be laid out with a view to their appearance in a picture but to their uses and the enjoyment of them in real life, and their conformity to those purposes is that which constitutes their true beauty. With this in view, gravel walks and neat mown lawns, and in some situations, straight alleys, fountains, terraces and, for aught I know, parterres and cut hedges, are in perfect good taste and infinitely more comfortable to the principles which form the basis of our pleasure in these instances, than the docks and thistles, and litter and disorder, that may make a much better figure in a picture.

Terraces around the house were now admired, serving as a plinth on which to set it, anchoring it, as it were, to the garden and landscape. They also served as an extension to the comforts of the house, for the public rooms were now generally on the ground floor, often had French windows or, even if still with sashes, opened directly onto the terrace. Arbours, seats, trellis-work, were all once again permissible, but only if they added to domestic comfort. Architectural show had no place. The house was thought of as the sun, its rays of comfort and refinement radiating into the garden, growing weaker as they went, until at the boundary of the garden 'pure nature' had sole power. Thus the garden was completely domesticized and no longer a stage set for hopefully Arcadian actors. People were at last content to be themselves. To show how far the reaction had gone, it is only necessary to look at the marvellous flower garden that Repton designed for Valleyfield in Fife. This had a central and straight canal, surrounded by flowerbeds and arbours. However, it was constructed within a short distance of quite a turbulent stream rattling down a steep-sided valley. The designed garden pays no attention whatever to the fine landscape around it. Contrast between artifice and nature was important for the first time in a hundred years. Valleyfield was much admired for both the house and the garden, but both are now vanished.

Near to the house, Papworth advocated frank artifice, even to fancy edgings for the flowerbeds.

This self-consciously 'primitive' Doric pavilion, built of logs and thatch, would have horrified architects and patrons of fifty years before.

For rather similar gardens, John B. Papworth published a number of quite extraordinary designs for garden buildings. With the beginnings of a new religious enthusiasm throughout the country, pagan temples, even if dedicated to the most proper of the ancient gods, were frowned upon. New excuses were needed for garden buildings, and so Papworth included designs for apiaries, laundries, ice-houses, even cenotaphs and Venetian tents. All these appeared in *Hints on Ornamental Gardening* of 1823. He himself had a very diverse career, embracing the post of Architect to the King of Württemberg, decorating the first paddle-steamer on the Thames and designing numerous small gardens. He worked at only two of the large ones; Claremont and Fonthill. He should also be remembered as the originator of the ineffable broken-column tombstone that became so popular in Victorian and Edwardian graveyards.

Hints was an immensely successful work, having vast sales in Europe where his architectural style would have found great favour, and also in Russia. His wildly neo-classical garden buildings are shown set amid luxuriant and very colourful plantings. Not surprisingly, he says, ". . . fashion is again adopting the aid of architecture and sculpture towards multiplying the means by which a judicious change and interest are created, in which she once abounded. . . ." The lawn, "a favourite auxiliary of every apartment on the ground floor", was to be decorated with flowerbeds of various shapes, interspersed with single evergreen trees or shrubs, together with an assortment of furniture that included "ornamental seats of china or porcelain, rustic or fanciful chairs, vases and basketwork borders to the flower beds". Tents, even marquees, were in general use throughout the summer. A garden that showed almost all these features, although not designed by Papworth, was the one at Deepdene owned by Thomas Hope (a member of the family with whom Repton had stayed in Holland). Hope, much more concerned with interior design (of which he was a very influential innovator), had a number of views painted of both his house and its gardens, the latter showing the new complexity and magnificence of the scene. Deepdene has gone, but parts of a Repton garden of entirely comparable magnificence remain at Woburn Abbey. The plans for this show how, once again, gardens were made up by assembling a multiplicity of small-scale elements. They were designed to cope with the new diversity of plant material and included a rosarium, various rockeries, a pinetum, other botanical gardens for plants from China and the Americas, plots for herbaceous plants, bulbs and evergreens, and a wide selection of greenhouses. For another sort of diversity, there was also an aviary and a zoo. How different from the gardens of only thirty years before; Arcadia had vanished.

George Johnson wrote in *The History of English Gardening* (1822): "Some persons without sufficient consideration have expressed the opinion that it [garden design] is now as near perfect as any Art can be, and therefore like all other human institutions it must now decline, since decay commences as soon as improvement ceases." Whether or not that is true, one symptom of decay was a growing interest in the 'art history' of gardening. An anonymous writer, calling him or herself 'Amateur', in the *Gardeners' Magazine* for 1829, after complaining that all garden layouts were becoming ridiculously similar whether for a London square or a country palace, wrote that one must examine the style of buildings and "give them gardens appropriate to their individual styles and eras of building [which] would . . . add truth and consistency to the character of each place, an object hitherto sadly neglected although generally allowed to be desirable. . . ." Having got so far, 'Amateur' then shows some ignorance of early garden styles, for the passage continues: "It would give also to the possessor an opportunity of introducing the description of garden ground I contest to be the best adapted to our climate. . . . It is a mistaken notion to suppose that because we enjoy not the climate of Italy, we cannot, therefore, appropriate to this country the Italian style of garden." And so it was Italy once more, and, as the Georgian Age faded, Victorian gardens sported all the mannerisms of Italian gardens, but with rarely much of the elegance and grace.

In 1833 the Director General of Gardens to the King of Bavaria wrote:

> Considered in respect to real landscape beauties, picturesque effects and grand imaginative characteristics, the English garden style is, in the present style, markedly retrograde. When I was in England in 1817, I found the gardens of the new English style, as I met with it, for the most part oppressed with the burden of their own ornaments. The immense multitude of plants which, since the commencement of the present century, have been brought from all parts of the world to Europe, and more especially England, supplies the landscape gardener with an inexhaustible fund for decorating his grounds. . . . The palette of the landscape painter, if I may so express myself, is now loaded with such a mass of colours and tints, that his means are superabundant, compared with the work of art he has to create . . . thus I found the English gardens a real chaos of unconnected beauties.

And so it remained for the next hundred years.

10. The British garden abroad

Horace Walpole, towards the end of his *History*, says:

> Truth, which, after the opposition to most revolutions, preponderates at last,
> will probably not carry our style of garden into general use on the Continent.
> The expense is only suited to the opulence of a free country, where emulation
> reigns among many independent particulars. The keeping of our grounds is an
> obstacle, as well as the cost of the first formation. A flat country, like Holland,
> is incapable of landscape. In France and Italy the nobility do not reside much
> and make small expense at, their villas. I should think the little princes of
> Germany, who spare no profusion on their palaces and country houses, most
> likely to be our imitators; especially as their country and climate bear, in many
> parts, resemblance to ours. In France, and still less in Italy, they could with
> difficulty obtain that verdure which the humidity of our clime bestows as the
> ground work of our improvements. . . .

This time he was wrong on almost all counts. The English style became the
rage all over western Europe and beyond; English gardens suddenly
appeared surrounding Russian palaces, as well as under the unsuitably
blazing skies of Sicily and Portugal. The style, however badly copied (and
Walpole eventually saw some terrible examples in France), was responsible
for the destruction of hundreds upon hundreds of ancient formal gardens
well into the nineteenth century, by which time the English were busy
rebuilding them. Because our style was so often used in unsuitable climates,
or on too small a scale, the beauties it vanquished were by no means
adequately replaced by anything of similar value. This was a matter for
regret to many British travellers before 1830, and perhaps it so remains.

Some of the earliest copies of English informality appeared in Sweden,
where the royal gardens of Drottningholm and Hage were given English
portions, designed partly by the cultured Gustavus III himself. Early
examples of about the same date are also found in Italy. Loudon, who visited
that country in 1819, found them to be far too ornamented. There was one
exception. Part of the landscape around the fabulous palace of Caserta, near

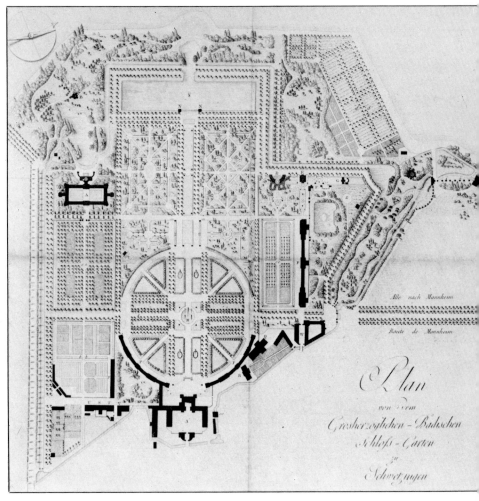

The gardens at Schwetzingen show an impressive formal core, with an 'English' landscape garden attached to the periphery.

Schwetzingen: the English style almost achieved.

Naples, was splendidly 'English'. It was, however, designed not by an Englishman but by a German gardener called Graeffer, although he did once have a nursery near London. He was also gardener to Lord Nelson at Brontë. In spite of the eminence of his connections, he was later murdered by peasants. At Caserta, as with a number of major gardens, only part was 'Englished'. The rest of the vast estate was left untouched, and the immensely long canal and its sequence of cascades was left fully in the Italian manner, with apparently no suggestion of turning it into a Brownian lake.

In Russia, the main examples of English gardens are to be found at the palaces near St Petersburg. The earliest was at the Peterhof, where a few winding walks were introduced only a few years after they had first been seen in their native land. Later, a gardener from the Duke of Northumberland's estate at Alnwick, a Mr Meader (who wrote vicious poems about both friends and enemies and eventually wrote two books, both largely plagiarized from Hill's *Eden*), designed a more advanced garden later in the century. The first major essay in the style dates from 1778, begun by Catherine II at Tsarskoe Selo. Modelled on Stowe, with that garden's heavy degree of embellishment, it included several exotic bath-houses and even a complete Tartar village that must have been the envy of some of the more sensational gardens in England. Plans of other Russian gardens, especially Oranienbaum and Pavlovsk (for which Brown was once thought to have supplied plans), show a curious hybridity of design. The innermost areas are all entirely formal, with major axes radiating out from the house. The outer parts of the gardens, or the interstices between the radial avenues, are filled with informal, and presumably later, designs.

A splendid example of an English periphery to a formal core is shown in Krafft's *Plans of the most Beautiful Picturesque Gardens in France, England an [sic] Germany. . .* published in all three languages in Paris in 1810. The immense and obviously sumptuous gardens at Schwetzingen, owned by the Duke of Baden, were widely admired. They must have been splendid to see from the network of canals that went straight or winding as necessary through the scheme. Other plans in Krafft's work show many examples of purely informal continental gardens. When they have relatively few garden buildings and contain tiny fields of wheat and barley or grapes, they were referred to as being in 'the English style'. As many of them were attached to town houses, the produce from the fields can scarcely have yielded more than a few loaves of bread and a bottle of wine. They seem to be a radical misinterpretation of Stephen Switzer's concept of the *ferme ornée*. Those gardens labelled as 'picturesque' would have appalled Uvedale Price. They were crammed with so many garden buildings that to go from one to the next scarcely needed a breath of air. A small garden near Rouen contained, as well as canals, basins and fish-ponds, a reading-room (in which to read

Rousseau's novels), a cottage, a hermitage and an observatory. Pressure on space was so strong that various garden buildings were often combined back to back, or one on top of the other, so that on one approach it might seem a rustic cottage and on another, a classical temple or a stony grotto. Some were very bizarre.

In France, no English garden pre-dates 1762. (Patriotism affects fashion.) The only really fine example of the style was at Ermenonville. The Marquis de Girardin had visited both Shenstone and Whately in search of the purest style, and the garden he created, with some assistance from the landscape artist Mahier, was greatly admired, although even in it a number of formal rides were left in the surrounding forest. It remains famous for the tomb of Jean Jacques Rousseau, which stands on a willow-girt island in the lake. According to Loudon, Girardin 'kept a band of musicians, who constantly perambulated the grounds making concerts sometimes in the woods, at other times on the water, and in scenes calculated for particular seasons . . . at night they returned to the house and performed in a room adjoining the hall of company'. The company themselves must have looked quite splendid, as family and guests had to wear a country uniform, with Madame Girardin and her daughters dressed in 'common brown stuff, *en amazone*, with black hats'. One hopes that the musicians were well paid for their strenuous work.

Krafft illustrates a very famous garden, the Petit Trianon at Versailles, the plan of which shows how tortured the English style could become in French hands. Patrick Neill, a Scotsman who will be mentioned later in these pages, visited the Petit Trianon in 1817. He describes how all the details are crowded together with not an idea of composition or expense, and suggests that the style is really *anglo-chinois*. The sense of surfeit is certainly not English: ponds, islets, waterfalls, cascades, rockwork, grottoes, caverns, huts, sylvan recesses, winter alcoves, groves of trees, thickets of underwood, spreading lawns, artificial hillocks, temples, obelisks. . . . He concludes that "the picturesque has everywhere been aimed at, and certainly not without effect!" Even today, with so much of it vanished and the rest romantically overgrown, there seems a glut of incident. Then, it must have been a relief to turn into the gardens of the Grand Trianon, wholly French, perfectly formal and utterly successful.

Neill also visited Malmaison, still in the state to which it had been reduced after its sack by the Prussian cavalry. The grounds had been designed first by Morel, then recast by Blaikie, a Scotsman who had worked in France for most of his life. The Revolution seems to have affected him very little, for although he had worked for the highest members of the aristocracy before it, it was he who supplied the potatoes planted in their lawns during it. He had to stay in France when he retired: he could not afford to come home, for neither the aristocrats nor the revolutionaries had

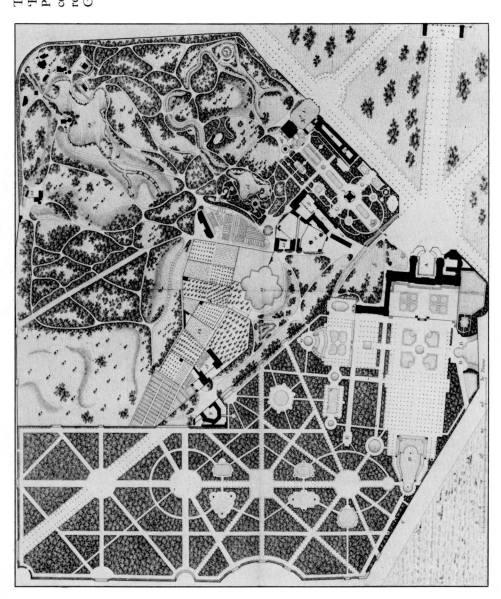

The congested plan of the 'English' garden of the Petit Trianon (Versailles) contrasts with the more relaxed formalism of the Grand Trianon gardens.

paid his fees. (Incidentally, the garden of the British Ambassador in Paris was, perhaps as a matter of politeness, in the French style.)

Neill also visited gardens in Holland and what is now Belgium. Only the one at the Château de Schoemberg, near Brussels, was at all good, but Neill found many of the other gardens so intriguing that he was almost converted to formalism. In almost every garden some 'anglicisms' had been added; those at Ghent owned by Baron Dubois de Vroeylande had rolling lawns that partly buried the trunks of trees that pre-dated the change. To achieve extent, the Baron had expanded his garden across a right of way, and so the villagers' cows were led across the garden with wicker muzzles to stop them eating the plants. Also near Ghent was a superb collection of American plants laid out in variously shaped 'English' clumps. The climate, more suited to them than anything in England, let alone Scotland, had produced superb specimens of magnolias, hydrangeas, rhododendrons, kalmias, andromedas and the rest of the now so popular *Ericaceae*. Sumptuous in another way, and one which bowled the moderately well-off Scot quite over, were the gardens of Madame Vilain XIV. Her beautiful château, moated, had a glazed bridge over the water that linked the reception rooms to an immense glasshouse, filled with pictures, statues, many mirrors, sofas, potted oleanders, passion-flowers and araucarias. From there, she could look over serpentine canals, comma-shaped beds of the rarest flowers, chinoiserie temples perched on tri-radial bridges, pagodas and a splendid Palladian bridge with marble columns, sphinxes and windows (unclassically) of stained glass.

Perhaps the oddest estate of all was near Antwerp, laid out in 1752 in an entirely hybrid way. While clipped hedges and topiary urns stood near the house, further away there were lakes and pagodas, a Chinese bridge, even a real Chinese junk on one of the wiggly canals. On emerging from one of the winding paths through the wilderness, Neill found himself on the edge of an open lawn, sunny, almost English. He believed himself looking at a perfect Arcadia, with about thirty sheep grazing quietly. None of them turned to look at him, for they were carved in stone!

Plants, gardeners and other elements

11. Fashion and fancies

Modern catalogues of seeds or plants usually group their contents under a number of well-known broad headings. Trees, shrubs, herbaceous plants and bulbs are the usual, and very functional, groupings. These divisions have a remarkably long history, and the growth of the science of botany from the beginning of the eighteenth century to the present day has done nothing to alter them. Only the emphasis on each section has altered to suit the aesthetic tastes and economic needs of the day. Culinary plants have always been listed separately, at the front of catalogues from the north of Britain (where gardeners were perhaps more interested in garden economics than beauty) and after decoratives in the south. Some London nurseries did not bother to stock plants for the kitchen garden at all.

Before dealing with the broad groupings in more detail in the following chapters, and the parts they played in garden design, it is worth saying something about fashions for plants and the way these fashions changed, not so much in response to the changing styles of gardening but in relation to the immense growth of species known, the technological possibilities of the garden and the more general tides of interest to which all fashions are subject.

William Cobbett, in his *American Gardener* of 1821, wrote, "That there is a great deal in rarity is evident enough, for while the English think nothing of the hawthorn, the Americans think nothing of the arbutus, the rhododendron, the kalmia and hundreds of other shrubs which are amongst the choicest in England." He went on to point out that golden-rod was the rankest weed in America but was grown in the grandest herbaceous walk in Europe (at Hampton Court), and our common corn poppy was a prize for all American gardeners. There would be no such thing as rarity if to collect things was not a widespread human need, and one felt by rich and poor alike. Gardeners who are also collectors may become botanists, people for whom the beauty of a plant is subordinate to a knowledge of its species and genus and its relationship to other plants. With them we are not concerned. Where visual pleasure is the most important factor, many are limited by their means as to what they can collect and maintain.

Almost throughout the Georgian period, as today, the rich could buy the rarest and most difficult plants from the furthest corner of the earth (indeed, the richest could afford to send out their own collectors to find them). The less well-off made do with simpler plants and, rather than search for new species, were naturally more interested in new varieties (now more correctly called 'cultivars') of plants already familiar. Even in this field, the latest varieties fetched much higher prices than those widely known. Although Britain never had anything comparable to the tulip mania seen in seventeenth-century Holland, prices could be high when compared with the wages of a head gardener or a cook. The now humble auricula (then called 'boar's ears', not 'dusty miller') is a case in point. This was extremely popular throughout the eighteenth century, and even by 1818 Loudon devotes several pages to its culture in the *Encyclopaedia of Gardening*. When James Justice's collection was broken up towards the end of the eighteenth century, some of the more beautiful plants fetched seventeen guineas each. (At that time a head gardener earned only twice that a year, and a minor gentleman could live on three hundred.) The owners of such expensive plants were naturally very jealous of them and anxious that propagation should not detract from rarity and price. Nevertheless, the best ones almost always found their way into general commerce, and in the early nineteenth century some London nurserymen stocked over two hundred types. Many of these were so fine that Dutch nurserymen, while scorning most other British productions, came to London to buy their own stocks.

Another early fancy, and one in which the Dutch remained master, was for the hyacinth. Regarded as one of the principal beauties of the spring, the range of colours was quite as large as that of today, and there were also many double varieties that have now disappeared. They were grown in pots or glasses for the house, or were planted outside in the same regimented plans still seen in the parks of seaside towns. The charming pink was also an enthusiasm of the same date, although it only became really popular after 1750. Like the auricula, it was very much a poor man's flower, almost never seen in the gardens of the rich. It was especially popular in the Midlands, and even more so at Paisley, where the first society devoted to its breeding was formed. It was said that much of the intricacy of pattern seen in Paisley shawls was developed from that seen in the chequered petals of the pink. While the collectors at Paisley recognized the existence of more than three hundred distinct varieties, only two hundred of these entered general commerce. It would be interesting to discover how many of these still exist in the gardens of industrial cities. In larger gardens, there were more general vogues, especially for plants with evergreen or variegated leaves, but these will be discussed in later chapters.

By 1800 a number of fancies were well established that have a very modern ring. Important gardens boasted fine collections of orchids and cacti, of dahlias, chrysanthemums and ferns. A passion for roses and rose-breeding had begun, and rose gardens as a particular part of the garden were becoming popular. Indeed, the rose was probably the most fashionable flower of all. Various species had been grown since remotest antiquity, but even by 1739 only fifty sorts were available for the garden. By 1780 systematic production of new types had begun, largely in France and Italy where the long summers ensured that ripe seed was produced. One Englishman who set up a nursery in France that specialized in roses claimed to have nine hundred sorts. Every season saw new productions, and by the early 1820s some of the London nurseries had lists almost as large. Loddiges of Hackney stocked, in 1830, more than fifteen hundred sorts, including many new Chinese hybrids. The introduction in 1786 of the four Chinese floribunda-type roses, with their double-flowering season, gave a great impetus to rose-breeding. The crosses with European roses gave rise to the hardy perpetual type that were in flower from June to the first frosts. It is difficult to believe that all these new sorts were distinct. Even the main nurseries of Glasgow and Edinburgh listed three hundred varieties, one Glasgow nursery claiming them all to be cultivars of the Scots rose (*Rosa spinosissima*), a species of which Loddiges had only half that number. No catalogue seems to have given any description of its contents, so gardeners must have gone to the nurseries to see what they wanted to buy.

While many of these early varieties have been lost forever, a few are still available, many of charm and some of great beauty. Interest in them seems to be reviving (perhaps the glaring charm of the hybrid teas is at last beginning to pall), and perhaps a number will be rediscovered as tangled thickets in old gardens.

Roses, if not in a 'rosarium', were usually planted in front of shrubberies or, in early-Georgian gardens, along the walks in the wilderness. The rosarium was usually planted in rather a formal way, with similar types of rose planted together to show their minute differences. The centre of such an arrangement was often occupied by a piece of 'rockwork' (forerunner of the rockery), on which pendant and dwarf types of rose were grown. Larger roses were trained as standards, which were used as single specimens on lawns or to form a small-scale avenue along the walks through the flower garden, exactly as in suburban gardens today. One interesting use which could return was the 'basket of roses', circular or rectangular beds edged with wire basketwork and the earth inside built up into a mound. A number of plants of one variety were put in, and, as they grew, stems were arched down and pegged to the earth. Eventually a tight and floriferous sheet of roses was formed, although weeding such an impenetrable tangle must have been a problem.

The illustrations of Miller's *Gardeners' Dictionary* were all of high quality and often of new species.

For the gardener who was interested in new species rather than in new types of old species, the entire period from 1730 to 1830 was one of continual, indeed increasing, excitement. The first part of the first edition of Philip Miller's *Gardeners' Dictionary* appeared in 1731 (dedicated, by the way, to Lord Burlington), and while one could undoubtedly plant a most interesting garden using just those species listed, Miller states in the eighth edition of 1768 that, since his work first appeared, the number of species available has doubled. Loudon estimated that in 1700 there were perhaps a thousand species grown that were not native to the British Isles. One hundred years later there were six times as many. Only twenty years on again, Loddiges listed in their catalogue nearly a quarter of the then known flora of the entire globe. This included about four and a half thousand hardy species, of which one hundred and eighty were ornamental trees, and more than twice that of herbaceous plants. Three thousand species were listed for unheated greenhouses, and fifteen hundred for heated ones.

Returning to the *Gardeners' Dictionary*, the illustrations (dedicated to John, Duke of Bedford) appeared from 1755 to 1760. This was more or less in the middle of the work's history, for the final edition (by then under the editorship of Dr Martyn) appeared in 1807. Many of the plates were the first ever illustration of the species shown. The first *Kalmia* introduced had just flowered and was given a plate, as were the first few magnolias. These had been sent from South Carolina and Georgia and were flowering at Goodwood. *Arctotis* had just been sent from the Cape, and a new *Bignonia* species from Virginia. The walls at Claremont were already draped with the marvellous flowers of *Bignonia radicans* (now *Campsis radicans*). The handsome tree *Robinia hispida* was still a great rarity in some London gardens, although by the early nineteenth century it was recommended for quick hedging or even as a quick way for growing firewood. A surprising number of succulents were already grown, and several plates were devoted to rare mesembryanthemums from the deserts of South Africa, representing plants now assigned to the genera *Faucaria* and *Cylindrophyllum*. There was at that date nothing from China or Japan, little from India and not a great deal from the nearer Orient or South America. Fifty years later plants were pouring into London from every continent, although even by the end of the period there were, by today's standards, few rhododendrons or azaleas (by 1830 there were only forty in each group available on the market), no forsythias and only two or three philadelphuses.

Amid such plenty it was no wonder that gardeners tended to specialize their interests. For some, of course, rarity was enough, and there were many books that illustrated the latest horticultural treasures. Roger Morris's marvellous *Flora Conspicua* of 1825 has already been mentioned, but there were many other examples, from the magnificently illustrated *Temple of Flora* by John Thornton to lesser part-works such as William Curtis's

Spring water, and garden architecture like Indian, but placed with only a few Indian species.

Botanical Magazine from 1787 (and still going splendidly) and Loudon's own *Gardeners' Magazine*. It was fortunate that advances in printing and colouring techniques coincided with such an upsurge of interest in the brilliantly coloured flowers from abroad.

A vogue for plants from America started in the second half of the eighteenth century and continued well into the nineteenth. The largest collection was William Beckford's at Fonthill, and, in spite of the scandals concerning the man, everyone wanted to see his stupendous garden. The American garden alone covered many acres; the rest was big enough to contain twenty-seven miles of rides. All American gardens were ancestors of the modern peat garden and were founded on a curious misconception of the American environment, and one related to the early exploration of that continent. All contemporary garden books insist that such a garden should be constructed of soil taken from marshes and bogs and that it should be mixed with dead leaves and fresh dung to a depth of three feet. Owners of ground already in this condition were considered very lucky. The reason for this curious soil recipe was that most plant-hunters in the Americas in the third quarter of the eighteenth century explored the country along the easy means of access, the rivers. It would have been natural to make collection easy and gather plants and seeds from the swampy lands at either side. It was only early in the next century that plants from other sorts of terrain (especially the mountains of the West) began to be extensively grown. Those were the years that saw an enormous number of conifers introduced, and which were to make such an enormous impact on the appearance of both gardens and the countryside at large. By then, too, American gardens could contain several magnolias and rhododendrons, kalmias, catalpas, arbutuses, vacciniums, cranberries (not much used in English cooking but extensively in American), andromeda, daphnes, bird cherries and that now most frequent denizen of the peat garden, the erica. In fact, no ericas came from America, but that did not seem to matter. Loddiges stocked more than thirty hardy European ones and three hundred and more tender ones from the Cape.

Few other countries seem to have given rise to a whole fashion in garden plants, although a few collections were made of Chinese plants (especially at Woburn Abbey) and then usually associated with garden buildings such as pagodas or dairies. A few Indian species were grown at Sezincote, of which some splendid watercolours were made by John Martin in 1810. Both countries have a vast number of plants quite as beautiful and tractable to horticulture as anything in America, and trade links were often quite as strong. The lack of specific collections is surprising, especially as America had no architectural idiom that could be copied for houses or pavilions in English gardens. Georgian architects had no knowledge of Aztec or Mayan buildings, though it would have been fascinating if they had. Brighton might have had a ziggurat rather than a Hindu pavilion.

12. Trees

Nothing, except the physical shape of the landscape, plays a more important part in landscape gardening than the trees which grow in it. Trees form, as it were, the secondary structural element, and, where the land is flat, the primary one. Today, trees have become somewhat divided into two classes: decorative ones for gardens and useful ones for the forest. In the Georgian period there was virtually no such distinction, except perhaps early in the nineteenth century when small suburban gardens were planted with small suburban trees. Apart from that late development, in those more expansive days, even the homes of the middle class had gardens of a size that would allow forest trees to grow unfettered.

There were also fewer purely decorative species available. Timber of almost every sort played a much greater part in everyday life than it does now. In country districts, some people still ate from wooden trenchers with wooden implements (all made from sycamore). The framework of all agricultural machinery was made of wood. Bark was used for tanning and dyeing and for heating greenhouses, and the inner bark provided cheap fibre matting. Charcoal was necessary for smelting and making gunpowder, and both it and timber were extensively used for domestic heating. Leaves were fed to pigs and used as compost or for heating melon-houses and stoves. Pumps and waterpipes were made of oak, elm or alder. Butter-firkins and flour-barrels were made of ash, and well-buckets were made of oak. All forms of transport, whether carriage, ship or sedan-chair, were built almost entirely of wood. Houses contained immense quantities of joinery, and of course all furniture was wooden. Furthermore, as the above list suggests, each type of timber had a particular property, and so almost every sort of tree had a value (except the horse-chestnut, which was useless for everything). Few gardens and certainly no parks were planted without the future value of the contained timber being a major consideration.

The planting of trees was seen as a national necessity throughout the period and indeed became something of a patriotic mania. The basis of this was the need for ships, for trade, defence and aggression. William Marshall wrote that a naval ship of seventy-four guns needed, in oak alone, about two thousand trees of two tons each, with crooked and straight wood in equal quantities. The keel would be of elm or beech, and the upper decks of deal. The outer underwater planking was of oak, too, but as Britain rarely produced wood of sufficient quality, it had to be imported. The masts and spars were of deal, and the rigging tackle of box, good elm or lignum vitae. Marshall estimated that fifty acres of oaks were needed, with about a hundred years of growing time at least. Consequently, many estates produced timber as their major crop, and it only needed the rides cut through the forest to be terminated with an obelisk or pavilion for them to form effective extensions to the garden proper. An extant and marvellous example of such an arrangement is still to be seen at Cirencester Park, largely designed by Earl Bathurst, although probably with assistance from Alexander Pope, whose favourite retreat it was.

These garden forests must not be thought of as drear and monotonous like the monoculture forests often seen today. They were planted in the spirit, already discussed, of Switzer's *Ichnographia Rustica*, and very much the spirit of the age: *in utile dulce*. A typical example of such planting was made by the Duke of Portland in Nottingham Forest (his head gardener was William Speechley who wrote a splendid treatise on the pineapple to be described later). Here, cedars of Lebanon were planted in irregular groves, interspersed with groves of beech, larch and Spanish chestnut. The cedars were used for panelling, the beeches (with a brittle and easily rotted timber) for cheap furniture and as firewood, the larches (as valuable as the best pine) for fencing and gateposts or wherever waterproof timber was needed, especially in dams and lock gates. Larch bark was very much valued by the tanners. Wood from Spanish chestnuts had all the same uses as oak and was much prized by the cabinet-maker. If the tree was coppiced, the poles were used for hurdles and barrel hoops. The nuts were eaten, and the bark also found its way into the tanning pits. The most widely planted tree of all was the oak, with birches used as the nurse crop. The Duke of Portland, perhaps considering their diversity not enough, also planted thousands of tulip trees (*Liriodendron*), and the rides were irregularly planted with hollies, yews, laurels and junipers. Apart from those at Nottingham, there were other magnificent cedars at Whitton Park, Warwick Castle and Painshill, all admired for this age. By that date, there were more cedars in England than were left in Lebanon. The tulip tree and the larch were both introduced in the seventeenth century.

Much wider ranges of species were found in some of the other well-known woods and gardens. By 1735 Woburn Farm had liquidambars, hemlock spruces, many types of acacia, hickories, pines, alders and cypresses. Painshill, larger and far more beautiful, and now being cropped for its timber, had all those as well as many American oaks, ilices, tupelo trees (the rarely grown *Nyssa sylvatica* which colours so splendidly in autumn), many types of poplar, as well as some of the first rhododendrons introduced. At Strawberry Hill, Horace Walpole had a surplus of trees from his nursery and offered them to his friends. Those who accepted his offer could have had Weymouth pines, arbor vitae, stone pines, black spruce, caroline cherries (probably a *Cornus*), laburnums, acacias, Virginia cedars and various firs (an ambiguous word for he included here the Scots pine).

Many of these species had commercial uses, although the acacias (probably species of *Gleditschia*, now spelt *Gleditsia*) and the *Cornus* had none that I have found. Of the pines, the Scots was much prized when grown in Scotland; if from further south, the wood was too coarse. The swamp pine (*Taxodium distichum*), another seventeenth-century introduction, produced planking that was more valuable than any other except that from the black larch. The Weymouth pine, introduced in 1705, was also used as planking; the pinaster was used for roof shingles (especially for early-nineteenth-century 'Swiss' cottages), and it was considered an especially good landscape tree. Some large specimens at Culzean were famous. Ironically, only the stone pine, the species most often seen in Italian landscapes and landscape paintings, gave poor wood. The various spruces, giving the timber called 'deal', were also used to make beer, the tender branch ends being used as the flavouring. It is not known if the vast specimens at Hatfield, Blenheim and Temple Newsam would have been used for this purpose. The balm-of-Gilead, described by Loudon as neither useful nor ornamental (for he had probably seen no large specimens), was grown for its resin, which, in the same manner as turpentine, was used medicinally. Few of the exotic oaks, and there were forty species available by 1800, were of much economic importance except to the tanning and dyeing industries. As the modern match was not yet invented, the poplars, too, were of little use. Lord Sheffield did advocate their use in furniture, for the heartwood has the colour and finish of mahogany. Of trees now regarded as entirely decorative, the laburnum was very highly valued for its very dark and very finely grained wood. The holly was used for a white veneer used in marquetry, and the various species of *Robinia* were also sought after by cabinet-makers. Loudon, ever prosaic, thought that because every member of the genus grew extremely fast, they would soon become a major source of fuel. That never happened. The ones that survived this suggestion are now extremely handsome.

While huge estates grew their own saplings from seed collected from notable trees (a knowledge of the powers of selection was current long before any theory of evolution), there was an extensive trade in saplings. As many southern landowners believed, wrongly, that seedlings raised in the north were more hardy and more easily established, million upon million of seedlings were shipped south from Scottish ports. One near Edinburgh produced and shipped to London two million seedlings a year. Another, in Aberdeen, produced larches, Scots pines, birches and alders. The larches cost about five shillings for one thousand one-year-old seedlings, but eight to nine shillings for a dozen at two years. Ash and beech were three to four times as expensive. It became very profitable to collect seed of almost any species (most spruce seed fetched ten pounds a hundredweight). Only a few of the nurseries were reliable; most planted the seeds so closely that the seedlings were weak and spindly and rarely survived. Nevertheless, the passion for planting was so intense that most agricultural and horticultural societies gave quite valuable prizes to whichever local landowner had planted the largest number of new trees.

Although most people who have visited the gardens of great houses will be familiar with the clumps and belts designed by 'Capability' Brown and his imitators, gardens of the 1730s are much less familiar. The many views of the gardens at Chiswick show walks and alleys bounded by low hedges (usually of hawthorn, produced from seed and planted at twelve-inch intervals) beyond which can be seen plantings of young trees. These areas, called 'wildernesses', fell out of use from the 1740s, until once again fashionable under Victoria. Some part of the garden had had this title since antiquity, and the 1739 edition of Miller's *Dictionary* described under that heading: "In the planting of these trees there are two principal things to be regarded; the first is to dispose them in such a manner that the different colours of the leaves may appear in some sort like the light and shades in a picture. The second is that the different manner of growing may be considered and so placed as to make so many irregular breaks in the plantation, as the size of the ground may admit." The first edition, under the same heading, described an entirely formal arrangement, and Miller tries to get over this solecism by saying, "I did not thereby mean to have whole lines of the same sort of tree, but as many sorts of tree as the soil and situation would admit." No doubt he did mean in lines, or in quincunx (a geometrically planted grove), a small area of which can be seen in almost every seventeenth-century garden illustration.

For the gardener who really did want to emulate the light and shade of a painting, the palette listed by Miller was remarkable. He divided trees into evergreens and deciduous, and each sort into three size divisions, some of which now seem questionable. He may well not have been aware of how high many of the new imports could actually become. For wildernesses large enough to hold the largest trees, there were over forty deciduous species and nineteen evergreens. Of middling-sized trees, there were many acacias (*Gleditsias* and *Robinias*) and numerous maples, although not the nasty Japanese type now so commonly grown. There was also *Styrax*, now rare in spite of the lovely flowers, five species of *Celtis*, as well as many hollies, bays and laurels. Some of the conifers included are now among some of the tallest trees in the country. For the small wilderness, or the edges of a large one, numerous species were suggested. One of the most unusual was the beautiful American persimmon, *Diospyros virginiana*, which colours so marvellously in autumn. There were also various privets (even then), mulberries, several *Rhus*, quinces, figs, almonds, coluteas (the senna pod now found on railway embankments) and the three then-known types of lilac, including the too rarely seen (and smelled) Persian lilac. A well-planted wilderness must have been a charming place indeed. The walks of sand or gravel were only four or five feet wide, and, as the main planting began at the same distance from the path, they must quickly have become elegant and shady. Although Miller discusses the use of hedges in great detail, the fashion to have them enclosing both the wilderness and its paths was in decline, and he suggests instead an informal planting of honeysuckles, roses and a number of other scented shrubs.

The irregular breaks in the plantations were often, as we have seen, accented with some architectural decoration. Whether it was a seat or a temple, the planting was carried out to show them off to the best advantage. Pope planted vistas in his garden so that trees with dark or bluish-hued leaves were furthest from the spectator's first view. This enhanced the feeling of recession, thus increasing the garden's apparent size, and also served as a fine foil to whichever obelisk or urn terminated the walk. Kent may have been suggesting something similar, for he frequently drew his gardens' buildings backed by conifers, if of a rather generalized sort, for he was clearly no botanist. This concern continued right through the period, and even Repton discusses it. His main concern, though, was whether gothic buildings should be set amid conifers, and classical ones in broad-leaved ones, or vice versa. He illustrates both states, trying to show that gothic buildings do not suit conifers. I do not feel that he proved his point; neither sort of building looks good among conifers. He did say, on the side of sense, that it was foolish to try to use vegetation in the same way as the painter uses paint. No artist would use colours that changed radically with the weather or the season. Repton realized that the form of a tree was more important. Miller's work was the first which gives lists of trees classified by their shape, although the difference between pyramidal and conical is perhaps no longer as clear as it may have been.

When 'Capability' Brown became the most sought-after designer of the day, the planting of trees underwent a profound change. Although the range of species available was continually augmented throughout the period of his influence, the numbers that played a part in the formation of the garden landscape became less and less. Simplicity was all. Trees grown for their flowers were banished to the flower garden. However, the balance was soon redressed. Nothing could stand in the way of the curiosity about the many

Kent backed his garden buildings (at Holkham) with generalized conifers.

Repton tried to persuade his readers that classical buildings looked better surrounded by conifers.

spectacular introductions. So much was available. The handsome *Rhododendron arboreum*, first introduced from Nepal by Captain Hardwicke in 1796, was soon lost and had to be reintroduced by 1817. This time it flourished (well, more or less, for it is hardy only in the south) and was soon in use as a lawn specimen or added to the inhabitants of the American garden. Of the correct nationality were several new magnolias, although the first of that genus (*M. glauca*) was growing at Fulham by 1688. The American Indians were said to use it to cure colds and chest complaints; the fruit was steeped in brandy, or the branches were boiled in water and taken as a tea. This never seems to have been adopted in England, most gardeners preferring to have both colds and their magnolias.

Repton seems not to have been much of a plantsman. His suggestions in the various Red Books, though colourful, were rarely botanically adventurous. Even for the subsidiary house that Mrs Burrell had built for herself in the grounds at Langley Park, he only suggested backing it with pines and laburnums. Evergreens were to be planted at the sides, in rather dark plantings of cedars, cypresses, Portugal laurels and arbutus. To lighten it somewhat, Repton suggested adding a few bird cherries, maples and planes. Nothing there that would speed the planter's pulse. In fact, it all sounds rather suburban, as if he had read Nicol's *Villa Garden Directory*, whose rather elaborate suggestions for making planting schemes correspond to social class are quoted in chapter 22. Whatever Nicol's social ideas, at least he planted with the latest introductions.

fir tribe and the yew, may succeed, being gradually blended with them, and so on. A similar grouping is observed in the herbaceous plants inserted in the front of the plantation; and the arrangement of the whole as to height, is the same as in the mingled shrubbery.

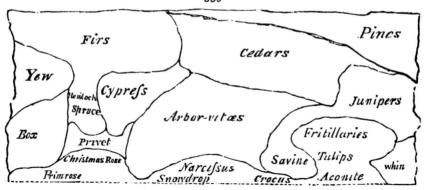

6142. *The chief difficulty* in this manner of planting is so to select the sorts that are to succeed each other, so to blend one group or kind with those adjoining, and at the same time maintaining the requisite gradation from the front to the back of the plantation, as to preserve to the spectator in walking along, the appearance of a *whole*. When this is successfully accomplished, and on a large scale, no kind of shrubbery can be more beautiful in summer ; but in winter it will present parts wholly without evergreens, and it will only be rich in flowers in some parts ; as for example, where the roses, spireæ, mespileæ, &c. are introduced. By proper contrivance, however, the evergreens the

This ambitious planting scheme is suggested by Loudon for a small shrubbery.

Loudon describes this grandiose shrubbery plan as being 'in the antique style'.

13. Shrubs

The word 'shrub' is so closely entangled with the word 'shrubbery' that it is very easy to imagine that they are of the same age. Yet there is no entry under 'shrubbery' in the 1739 edition of Miller's *Dictionary*, although a long and interesting series of lists are given for shrubs. However, it was well used by the time Loudon's *Encyclopaedia* appeared in 1822, where it is described in a very grandiose way. The recommendations for a small shrubbery include no less than one hundred and fifty species, some of which are large trees. He says very little about the best means of laying out this plethora of vegetation but does say that the usual method, where everything is indiscriminately mixed up, is not very satisfactory. Even the less ambitious shrubberies of today suffer from this weakness, but I am not sure that his suggested alternative, that of grouping plants by their botanical affinities, would produce beautiful plantings, however intellectually interesting it might be. In any case, few now have room for more than two or three species from any genus and could certainly not reserve parts of it as suitable for a mixture of pines and cedars.

Loudon's attempts to reduce the 'promiscuity' (his word) of planting rather obscure the origin of the shrubbery, which is really part of the old 'wilderness' reduced in size until it can fit into a suburban garden. Plants now usually considered denizens of the shrubbery were sought after long before shrubberies as such were planted, let alone become the dark and tangled, laurel-filled jungles that conceal so many late-Georgian houses from the public gaze. We are now very unfair to laurels, acubas and the rest. Once all evergreens were highly prized and loved, although long before the Victorian era draped them with sentiment and soot. Such plants were usually grouped together in a specialized area called 'the winter garden', thought of not as dark and funereal but as being bright and joyful. This was even more so if the plants had leaves spotted with white or yellow or had bright berries in the depth of winter. Other parts of both wilderness and shrubbery were planted for particular seasons as well. As Loudon suggests that even a small shrubbery should contain walks of at least a mile, there was little difficulty in accommodating a number of such areas.

However much pleasure such places were expected to produce, none was expected to make a profit. Early-eighteenth-century plantings often included the smaller types of fruit and nut trees, but only because these were often decorative in leaf, flower and fruit. They were grown in orchards for produce. In 1772 William Chambers described a fake Chinese shrubbery in the *Dissertation*. This consisted "of rose, raspberry, bramble, currant, lavender, vine and gooseberry bushes; with barberry, alder, peach, nectarine and almond trees . . .". A splendid shrubbery to eat one's way through, if the birds were shot out of it. Loudon would certainly have disapproved, for he regarded the inclusion of 'productive' plants as an intrusion on the general sentiments to be felt while meandering for exercise or pleasure, perhaps too gross a reminder of profit and money. Neither was to be thought of among the lilacs and hollies, spireas, viburnums, coluteas and spartiums or, in the more shady parts, daphnes and hypericums with ivy and periwinkle draped beneath them. (The gardener who once owned my copy of the *Encyclopaedia* must have had a very shaded garden indeed, for each of the species listed as suitable for shade is heavily underlined.)

Loudon also gives other specialized lists. Plants with scented leaves and flowers included *Salix viminalis* (the native osier) and *Betula sibirica*, as well as honeysuckles, jasmines, roses, azaleas and the very sweetly scented and too little grown *Clematis flammula*. Fruiting plants that would not remind the unwary sentimentalist of some of the coarser aspects of human life were junipers (if they knew nothing of gin), pyracanthas, vacciniums (excepting the edible ones), various *Berberis* (although the barberry was then used extensively in cooking, especially of hares), various *Sorbus* species, empetrums and vacciniums. Many of these are still in common use today, and indeed the late-Georgian shrubbery would not look in the least dated if one could see it today. Only the enthusiast would notice a number of absences, for there would be no forsythias or ceanothuses (perhaps *C. americanus* if it was very late), no glaring azalea hybrids, only a few rhododendron species, no mahonias, only five hydrangeas, nine cotoneasters and a single buddleia (*B. globosa*). Where large present-day shrubberies are occasionally hedged with privet or holly or the currently fashionable Lawson's cypress, Loudon adds olearias, rhamnuses, *Viburnum tinus* and even the late-flowering *Hibiscus syriacus* (known since the sixteenth century) and *Robinia hispida*. For edgings rather than hedgings, pinks and lobelias were then in use, as well as andromedas, empetrums and lavenders. However, the plant most recommended for such a position was the box, which had virtually vanished from gardens together with the parterre. The reappearance of *Buxus sempervirens* marks the end of the English landscape style, and a conscious return to the earlier glories of Italy.

Sixteenth-century Italy missed many pleasures and a few menaces. No garden of that date would have survived the onslaught of the snowberry (*Symphoricarpus rivularis*) introduced from Missouri in 1817 and soon a scourge in every garden. They would have welcomed *Rhododendron nudiflorum*, the splendid scarlet flowers of which were to become so popular. An illustration of this in *Flora Conspicua* has the appended prognostication, "Notwithstanding the many excellent properties and powerful attractions of the azalea tribe, they will, like the rest of the American shrubs, be most probably limited in their cultivation." Morris was very wrong. One planting scheme he suggested, was the mixing of the European *Rhododendron ferrugineum* with *Gaultheria procumbens*, the fragrant *Epigea repens* and various ericas.

If late-Georgian shrubberies would appear only slightly less highly coloured than those now being planted, the wilderness of a hundred years or so before would be rather stranger. The style of planting has already been described, most shrubs being restricted to the margins of the paths winding through it. While most native species found a place, many remarkably exotic-looking plants were also used, including a number that have unjustifiably dropped out of use. Of the largest bushes, the snowdrop tree (*Halesia* species), the beautifully flowered indigo trees (*Indigofera* species), various sumachs, although not the unavoidable purple-leaved *Cotinus coggyria*, and coluteas, are examples. The spicily scented benzoin tree (*Lindera benzoin*), with its fine autumn colours, as well as the azederach (*Melia azedarach*), deserves rehabilitation, even if the last would only 'do' in the south. As to climbers, whether to make the wilderness more truly wild and impenetrable or to clothe a wall or to entwine an arbour or an urn, by 1740 there were two species of *Bignonia* (only one now occasionally seen), several *Clematis* (none of the gaudy hybrids), ivies, passion-flowers, jasmines and menispermums (the wildly rampant moonseed) and the now unused wolf vine (*Vitis vulpina*). There was even the plant that must now occupy a larger acreage of wall than any other species, the Virginia creeper.

When the wilderness vanished, as it were, into the landscape, the residue became merely part of the pleasure ground. As such, its position and layout was often subordinated to the architectural needs of the house to which it was attached. As has been described earlier, the idea that a house should show clarity, symmetry and grandeur on all sides meant that the untidy cluster of supporting buildings had to be detached from it. In the middle of the period they were often so detached that they were given an architectural treatment of their own. This, though elegant, must have been very inconvenient, and the most obvious solution was to leave them attached to the main house but obscured in some way. The shrubbery offered an ideal means of doing this, obscuring the offices in a decent leafy shade while leaving a large part of the main block to flaunt its elegance and grace. There

This *cottage ornée* by Papworth shows how the garden began to obliterate the house.

were no trees that would eventually overshadow the works of man. Repton made a great deal of use of plantings in this narrowly architectural sense, and it was quickly realized that, at least for small houses, planting and architecture could be more closely combined. This was especially true of a house type called the *cottage ornée* (to be described in Chapter 22).

Until that moment the only buildings 'planted over' had been sham gothic ruins, to give them false age and somewhere for a few sinister owls to roost. No owner of a classical eighteenth-century house would have wanted a single leaf to cover up the expensively carved detail or the perfect proportions of his house. Only the burgeoning Romanticism of the early years of the following century, with its worship of exaggerated rusticity, would have thought of submerging a house entirely beneath vegetation. By the 1820s, a number of house plans had been published in which the house was designed almost as a flower-pot, with trellis-work pillars supporting the low eaves on which to entwine wisterias and honeysuckles, various species of *Smilax* and morning glories. Some houses even had pockets of earth built into the walls in which the roots of climbers could find sustenance. This must represent the ultimate triumph of horticulture over architecture. Not surprisingly, no examples have survived. Nevertheless, the idea, if not the plants, took root, and few Victorian houses were without ivied or creepered walls. Sadly, many proud and classical houses soon vanished beneath the prevalent greenery, and many so remain.

While urban gardens will be discussed in detail in a later chapter, it should be said here that shrubberies were admirably suited to urban scale. Few gardens behind the elegant terraced houses of the middle and late part of the period were large enough to hold full-sized trees, and even the larger gardens of circus and square could never pretend to landscape. Shrubberies were used to create internal spaces within these gardens that gave as much as possible an illusion of rural retreat. A number of these still retain elements of their eighteenth-century layouts, but there are very few of the individual house gardens that do. The pressure on the latter, especially of changes in fashion, are much greater. Because the public ones were owned, or at least regulated, by all those whose houses faced on to them, the money for wholesale alteration was harder to raise and radical changes of appearance much harder to implement. Incidentally, although most large nurseries were attached to urban centres, and the range of plants they stocked was large, the numbers of species that would thrive in urban conditions was quite small. Loudon has no hesitation in saying that no rose would grow in London. Evergreen shrubs and a few deciduous trees seemed to be all that would. It must be remembered that, in winter, most town houses would have at least five or six coal fires burning almost continually, and so the same number of chimneys would be belching smoke for every thirty or forty feet of street.

Most owners of gardens were interested mainly in shrubs that would happily (or only with the mildest coddling) survive the winter out of doors. For the opulent, with glasshouses of one sort or another, there were many tender species available. Surprisingly, some of these are now grown in the open without concern. An early collection could have included eighteen sorts of *Citrus*, various Mediterranean bushes such as *Phlomis* species, myrtles, absinthes, coronillas and teucriums, as well as more exotic plants such as the carob and various melianthuses. A late collection, and one at the apex of wealth, was that found in the conservatory of The Grange, one of the most extraordinary Greek Revival houses ever built. The collection contained some of the first proteas to flower in this country, the dramatic *Musa coccinea* (a scarlet-flowered banana), *Erythrina*, araucarias, many camellias, acacias and jacarandras. It must have been an impressive sight. It would not have smelled so good when the *Enkianthus* was in flower.

14. Flowers and the flower garden

John Claudius Loudon could, without qualm, write in 1819 that "it has been frequently observed that flower gardens have been on the decline for the last half century, and that the cause of this appears to have been the influx of new plants during that period, by which gardeners have been induced, without due consideration, to be more solicitous about rarity and variety than well disposed to colours and quality." While there may have been a decline visually, and after all, standards had been immensely high, the passion for flowers in all its aspects had never really abated. Indeed, it was to continue long after Loudon wrote those words, and today the word 'gardening' is almost commensurate with 'flowers'.

The flower garden has existed since early times. Its place in the more general garden has changed very much, and in ways that reflected every alteration in the gardening aesthetic of the day. Flowers had, of course, been one of the most important elements in the long border and the parterres of all but the most vulgar or the most subtle of formal gardens. In the former flowers were replaced by coloured stones or crushed glass; in the latter flowers were suppressed in favour of the many shades of green. In parterres that did have flowers, each section of the design was usually worked out with a single species of bedding plant, the different parts of each section having them in a different colour. Long borders often contained a mixture of perennials, bulbs and annuals only rarely planted in any formal sort of way. When the fashion changed and parterres vanished for a hundred years, for a good part of that time flowers were hidden in the shrubbery or behind the stone walls of the kitchen garden. Plainly, they were of no use in the open garden, where clumps of even the brightest flowers would hardly have registered in the wide spaces of the new landscape. Further, to grow flowers well needs artifice, and artifice itself was out of fashion. Walpole, for his *riant* garden, placed colourful plants along the edges of his plantations, and no doubt similar things happened in many of the smaller gardens. Nevertheless, the walled flower garden became the most important refuge for most herbaceous and annual plants throughout the English landscape-garden craze. Anyone looking at a flower garden today, with its blazing colours, its Fı hybrids, and the furious pace of introduction of new cultivars, could be excused for thinking that its eighteenth-century equivalent would have made, by comparison, a poor show.

This is very far from the case. A glance at contemporary garden catalogues or at almost any garden book will find a range of species quite as large as, if not larger than, even the most ambitious catalogues contain now. Certainly there were no immense blue delphiniums, cerise petunias or frilly snapdragons. The catalogue of Dirk and Pierre Voerhelm of Haarlem (much flower seed was imported from Dutch nurseries) lists an immense variety of material, a great deal of which is now found in cottage gardens. Amaranths, balsams, candytufts, geraniums, lady's smock, lavender, scabious, flax, lupins (Voerhelms sold only small blue variegated ones, or a yellow species), nasturtiums, tobaccos, many sorts of poppies, including the splendidly vulgar *P. orientale*, sweet williams, sweet sultans and double meadowsweet. There were also some rather unexpected plants: for instance, *Tordylium* was grown for its decorative seed pods, as were 'caterpillars', whose name explains the shape. Scarlet pimpernels were grown as decoratives, as were several grasses. The dried seed pods of honesty were used to fill empty fireplaces, and campanulas (especially *Campanula pyramidatum*) and asters were grown in pots to decorate courtyards and rooms.

Rather later in the period, Sir William Chambers's *Dissertation*, already quoted for his description of a "Chinese" shrubbery, also contains an interesting description of an equally "Chinese" flower garden, mysteriously stocked with all sorts of flowers from England. It is one of the few descriptions of a proposed planting scheme. He describes it in the following way:

> The Chinese gardeners do not scatter their flowers indiscriminately about their borders, as is usual in some parts of Europe, but dispose them with great circumspection and, if I may be allowed the expression, paint their way very artfully along the skirts of the plantation, and in other places where flowers are to be introduced. They reject all those that are of straggling growth, of harsh colour and poor foliage, choosing only such as are of some duration, grow either large or in clusters, are of beautiful forms, well leaved and of tints that harmonize with the greens that surround them. They avoid all sudden transitions, both with regard to dimension and colour, rising gradually from the smallest flowers to the hollioaks [hollyhocks], paeonies, sunflowers and carnations, poppies and others of the boldest growth, and varying their tints, by easy gradations, from white, straw colour, purple and incarnate, to the deepest blues and most brilliant crimson and scarlets. They frequently blend several roots together, whose leaves and flowers unite and compose only one rich harmonious mass; such as the white and purple candytuft, larkspurs and

mallows of various colours, double poppies, loopins [*sic*], primroses, pinks, and carnations, with many others whose form and colours accord with each other. And the same method they have with flowering shrubs. . . .

It would seem that a Chinese gardener must have stolen a look at the flower garden at Nuneham, so strong is the similarity. The garden there was designed by the poet William Mason, the same gentleman who published a violent attack on the *Dissertation*, called *An Heroic Epistle*, which had great success. The various dates are interesting. The *Dissertation* is of 1772, the *Heroic Epistle* from two years later, but the gardens at Nuneham date from about 1775, so it was not a Chinaman cribbing from there but Mason taking ideas from the man he attacked. Whatever the source of the inspiration, the garden was widely illustrated from 1777 and presumably widely copied. In 1783 Mason published his *English Garden*, an extremely long poem about almost every aspect of gardening. It does not have a great deal about flower gardens, but it does have the following awful suggestion, quoted here from the extensive 'notes' rather than the verse (see p. 171):

"For of genuine taste humanity is the inseparable associate. On the children, therefore, of the labouring peasants, we are previously desired to confer the charge of superintending all our boundaries and guarding them from the invasion of herds and flocks. In order to adapt them to this little stewardship, to change their weeds of poverty for a more cleanly and comfortable attire, and arming the infant shepherds with the proper implements of their picturesque office, to employ and post them where they may be even conspicuously seen . . .'.

While the disposition of plants at Nuneham (within walls, not a ring of 'infant shepherds') seems to have been as informal as Mason insists on all aspects of planting, only thirty years later Loudon advocates what seems, even now, a rather odd-looking planting scheme: "Flowers in borders should always be planted in rows, or in some regular form, and that this appearance should be assiduously kept up by trimming off all irregular side shoots and straggling stalks, and reducing the bulk of plants that grow too fast. . . ." Clearly, the trimmed and fettered plants of municipal flower beds have an ancient lineage. A garden where all such inhibitions were ignored was that belonging to the actress Mrs Siddons, whom all admired but who, from the evidence of her garden, must have been quite odiously melancholy. It is described with admiration in Hogg's *Treatise on Flowers* of 1812 and is held up as a splendid example of using large masses of a single species. The garden was "at her late residence in the Harrow Road [where] her favourite flower was the *Viola arvensis*, the common purple heartsease, and this she set with unsparing profusion all around her garden. . . ." No doubt a very gloomy place indeed, for the rest of the planting consisted of evergreens, particularly sombre ones like box, fir, privet, phyllyrea, holly, cypresses,

The frontispiece of Maria Jackson's *Florist's Manual* shows a formal design that looks quite modern.

A weakly informal plan of a late Georgian flower garden (from *The Florist's Manual*) looks rather like today's island beds.

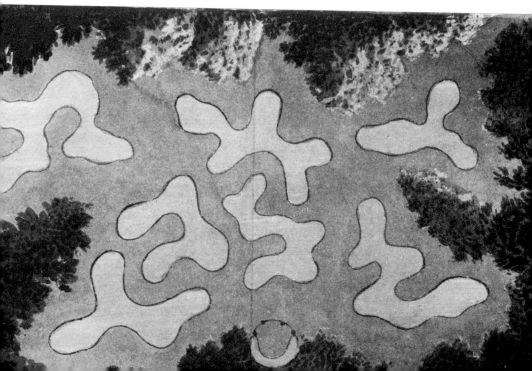

laurels, bays and so on. Patrick Neill, already alluded to, admired a similar simplicity of planting. "Nothing can be finer, for example, than to see many plants of double scarlet lychnis, double sweet williams or double purple jacobeas." That must have been nice, but we know that his own garden at Canonmills Cottage in Edinburgh was a jumble of plants, both native and exotic. There was a similar mixture of animals. (He listed its contents when appealing against a railway company's wish to lay their rails through it; he won.)

If the foregoing implies that some gardens, at least, were visually far more sophisticated than the sort of 'cottage garden' one might expect, garden accounts from various smaller country houses conjure up a fine picture of a relaxed and informal planting of simple flowers. In 1773 the owner of a Scottish example bought twenty sorts of annuals for ten shillings, which included Canterbury bells, 'bloody' wallflowers, stocks, asters, French marigolds, nigella, rose larkspur, white sweet sultans, mignonette and persicaria (*Polygonum* species). In 1820, the same gardens were sown with exactly the same plants, with the addition of scabious and yellow lupins, and unusually the 'sensitive' plant *Mimosa pudica*. There were also many herbs. Eight years later, the first dahlias were bought at a shilling each, with more of the usual annuals and biennials, by then costing two shillings for twelve sorts. Two dozen hollyhocks were bought for four shillings.

By the time these were planted, one of the first books exclusively concerned with the flower garden had been on the booksellers' shelves for four years. Written by Maria Jackson in 1822, it was entitled *The Florist's Manual, or Hints for the Construction of a Gay Flower Garden*. It gives a remarkably complete idea of what a late-Georgian garden of this type must have looked like, everything being described and illustrated in great detail, whether the garden was informal in plan or 'Etruscan'. She disliked borders of single species, feeling that everything must be mixed together. However, she enjoined that the gardener's energies should "not be for rare species but for new colour, so that the commonest primula which presents a fresh shade of red, blue, yellow, etc., ought to be esteemed more valuable than the most rare American plant which does not bring a similar advantage". Her own garden at Somersall Hall near Uttoxeter must have been bothered by snails, for she was very enthusiastic about her solution, which was to "strew pieces of turnip about. Snails prefer that to anything else, so the other plants are not eaten, and the snails may be gathered up and destroyed."

15. Exotics

The word 'exotic' covers a constantly changing range of plants. Most garden plants, not being native, are in a sense exotic, but the word is mainly associated with rarity and cost. Many species which have now vanished from gardens because every gardener has become bored with them may, fifty or a hundred and fifty years ago, have been expensive, sought after and considered highly beautiful. Some that were symbols of wealth and elegance (strelitzias, gardenias, most of the orchids) are still the flowers of the fortunate. Exotics, as we shall be concerned with them here, are exotic for two reasons: firstly, they were introduced from abroad at some point during the Georgian period (starting off with plants from the Americas and ending with a flood of species from Africa and the Orient), and secondly, because they were then considered as needing special conditions for their cultivation. Some still need them; others may not.

Only one genus of exotics, *Citrus*, grown since Roman times and still valued throughout the eighteenth century (some growing in France in the 1820s were reputed to be over four hundred years old), gave its name to a piece of architecture. Although the plants are now commonly grown on office windowsills, they were originally housed in magnificent orangeries. The first English examples date from the seventeenth century, and throughout the reigns of the Hanoverians the orangery diversified into a large number of forms adopted to genera other than *Citrus*. It was only the winter residence of the plants, when an open fire kept out the frost; in summer they were used as places in which to take tea or to dine. The orange or lemon trees, in white or green tubs, were arranged along terraces or gravel walks, or as part of an elaborate formal scheme, as at Chiswick in the 1730s. The first orangeries were not especially suitable places to grow plants, for the roofs were solid, and there were windows in only one of the sides, more rarely in three.

An orangery held more than oranges: there were thirty types of *Citrus* available in London nurseries that produced fruit. Only the grapefruit seems to have been missing. Most of the fruit was edible, although sometimes the flowers were sold off to perfumers. Other genera were soon taken into the orangery: myrtles, bays, some laurels and even oleanders. By 1739 the first camellias had been introduced, and selection and hybridization of the original red, white, single and double types started almost immediately. Advances in heating methods, described in Chapter 16, meant that by 1740 those who didn't mind the smell of rotting manure could in the depths of winter stroll beneath the leaves of fuchsias from New Spain, bananas (first flowered and fruited in England only a few years before), various tender species of magnolia, three types of vanilla orchid (imported because the Spanish used it to improve the flavour of drinking-chocolate), twenty or thirty sorts of grape, six varieties of pineapples (although these were first fruited in 1719 at Richmond), rare begonias, marantas and even rarer *Brunfelsia*. Their gardeners were just beginning a fight that still continues unabated that against the ravages of scale insect and mealy-bug. Both pests were new additions, the former beast just having decimated the sugar-cane plantations in the Caribbean, driving up sugar prices, making some men rich and ruining others. Recommendations were made for the planting of the immune cocoa tree instead, soon to produce a new crop of rich men. Each tree could produce about thirty shillings' worth of fruit a year.

Interest in succulents had started at the beginning of the eighteenth century (most of the first seed being sent from Holland), and Richard Bradley wrote the first book concerned entirely with them in 1716. There were soon some notable private collections. Interest was not confined to the genteel classes. In 1729, a rare aloe flowered in a London garden, and the whole world came to see it. One group of gentlemen began to attack it with their swords, and a servant who tried to prevent them was likewise assaulted. The plant's owner intervened a moment after and received a wound in the neck from which he never recovered. One hundred years later, with such dangers lessened, the list of species available was very large. Some are now very rarely seen in private collections but were then very common (especially the genus *Melocactus*) and were quite probably over-collected in the wild.

Drought resistant, but not so juicy, is the universally grown geranium (correctly *Pelargonium*). It was an enormously popular genus from the time its first representatives were imported at the end of the eighteenth century. Like many other xerophytes, many species came from South Africa and, like them, were much collected during the reign of George III. Geraniums were highly regarded for two reasons. Some could be had in flower all the year round, and this gave them a great advantage during the flowerless winters of the time. They were also crossed with ease to produce new varieties. New types, until they became widely grown, were as valuable as the Cape heath, a plant which has now fallen from favour. The South African ericas were

Lord Burlington's orange trees at Chiswick were set outside during the summer and added elegantly to the pleasures of the garden.

Loudon's scheme for an 'economic Botany' conservatory attached to a nobleman's palace.

The Grange, Hampshire, in the Doric style, with its immense Ionic conservatory to the left.

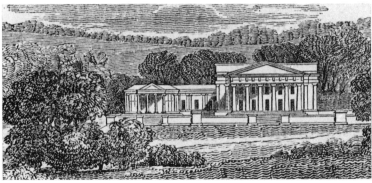

extremely fashionable. George III even financed collectors to explore the Cape to find new sorts. By 1819 there were more than two hundred and fifty available, in all colours and in flower at every season. Loudon gives an elaborate chart so that gardeners could select colour schemes for the 'heath house' for every month of the year. They were commonly illustrated in all the lavish gardening picture-books of the period.

While geraniums, heaths and other small plants were usually grown in pots on the slatted staging of greenhouses, the word 'conservatory' was generally used for a greenhouse where the plants were actually bedded out permanently. Unrestricted root room and plenty of growing space allowed even the most exuberant shrubs and climbers to grow decently. From the 1790s onward, the conservatory was often attached to the main dwelling-house. Importance was often placed on scented species, so jasmines were popular, as were hoyas and some of the other asclepiads. Passion-flowers and bignonias twined round support wires, and even the sinister and evil-smelling flowers of *Aristolochia*, or the equally dismal leaf-vases of *Nepenthes*, were admired. Gardenias, acacias (proper ones being introduced at the end of George II's reign, together with mimosas and eucalyptus), heliotropes, a whole range of African proteas and even a number of splendid and tender rose species, such as *R. indica* and *R. semperflorens*, were all grown. Curiously, *Fuchsia magellanica*, now grown even in the north of Scotland out of doors, was then treated as tender. *Flora Domestica, or the Portable Flower Garden, illustrated from the works of the Poets*, written in 1823 by Elizabeth Kent, suggested that it was especially suited to the morning-room or the study.

Many other plants were not just confined to the glasshouses; they played their part in the decoration of the main house as well. In the reign of George I, the range of plants used to embellish rooms was quite scanty. Hyacinths and narcissi were used in the spring, campanulas and various balsams in the summer, and occasionally tuberoses imported from Italy and Holland scented the air. Both tuberoses and balsams were to be used throughout the period. The *Gardeners' Magazine* of 1829 describes a bed of the latter growing in the garden saloon at Whitmore Lodge, where the red flowers looked fine against the brown walls and the bird's-eye maple woodwork. In the early part of the period, winter and autumn were rather bare, with a few evergreens brought indoors from the orangery. Rooms were, in any case, rather sparsely furnished, and plants did not play much part in their decoration. As the century progressed, more plants were found that could stand the rigours of house life: the dust, the wild shifts in temperature, and the sins of omission and commission of owner and gardener. Rooms, too, became more comfortably furnished, and plants, from the humblest to the rarest, were used to soften the cold formality of earlier times. The first gardening books to describe, in any great detail, cultivation of plants under these conditions all date from the early nineteenth century. William Nicol's *Villa Garden Directory* has a section on "the treatment of shrubs and flowers kept in the green-room, the lobby and the drawing-room", and the shrubs include such unlikely things as the spotted *Acuba japonica*, which might have looked quite handsome, the balm-of-Gilead (small specimens, no doubt) and the strawberry tree. Hydrangeas, balsams, camellias, fuchsias, lilies, yet more jasmines and geraniums were all possibilities. Many others rather presupposed the existence of a greenhouse or garden, for few would grow successfully indoors. Carnations, ericas, lobelia, daphnes, mignonette, proteas, stocks, rockets and wallflowers were all suggestions. Nicol places great emphasis on scented plants, and one must remember that bathing, even in the 1820s, was not as frequent as today. Clothes, too, were less often cleaned, for a garment of any complexity had to be completely dismantled before it was washed. An even moderately crowded drawing-room might well have needed every flower available. Nicol suggests that stocks could be used in working-class homes, where perhaps the perfume needed to be stronger.

As the big Georgian urban developments in London and other major cities were completed, receptions began to form a very important part of any householder's social life. A number of the larger nurseries began to rent out plants for the evening as decorations. They charged, on average, about 50 per cent of the plant's value. Although the risk of damage was high (curiously, many plants were killed by the heat), the trade was very profitable, and a number of nurseries became entirely devoted to it. Before the monkey puzzle tree (*Araucaria araucana*) was found to be hardy, there was a magnificent and valuable potted example at Kew. It was brought into Carlton House for a ball and went up in flames when servants hung lamps from its branches. While the plants in the house were often of the hardier sorts, the stove houses and bark houses (the latter were the warmer) often housed many species too delicate or too rare for such treatment. Here, as with conservatory plants, a number have been found to be tougher than expected. Perhaps it is just that the human inhabitants of the drawing-room have come to expect a more equable environment. The benjamin fig, the castor oil plant and the gardenia are often seen outside the greenhouse, even if crotalarias and many clerodendrons remain inside. Gloxinias and all begonias were once cosseted. Morning glories, *Cissus antarctica*, *Rhoicissus rhomboidea* and many bromeliads now grow splendidly in a sunny room. Even strelitzias, heliconias and gingers can be persuaded that they do not need more tropical conditions than a normal living-room can now provide.

Few tropical crop plants have much conventional beauty. Most botanical gardens have a collection of such species, but they are infrequently visited except by parties of schoolchildren with an enthusiastic biology teacher. The first published suggestion for such a collection can be found in

Loudon's *Encyclopaedia*. He believed that everything should be included, from soursop to calabash, cocoa to cashew (the latter then with medicinal, as well as culinary, use), pawpaws (both for the fruit and for the papain even then used for tenderizing meat), cinnamon, vanilla and the rest. He suggested that wealthy patrons should form those collection for the edification of young travellers, for "our connection with these (colonial) countries, and the number of young persons that annually leave Britain to pass the greater part of their lives in them, it is desirable that those plants should be known here also, and hence a rational object for the patriot who has wealth and leisure to display them in a conservatory attached to his castle, or palace, of suitable elevation and extent". How earnest this, and how it prefigures the intenseness of Victorian Britain; how grandiose, too, are Loudon's designs for it.

16. Glass

The word 'glass' was used throughout the eighteenth century in a generic sense to cover all sorts of frames and greenhouses and is used today in exactly the same sense, even if the range of types of 'glass' is rather more prosaic. Nowadays, even if greenhouses are used to produce lettuces or tomatoes, carnations or Peruvian lilies, they are unlikely to be designed specifically for the needs of a particular crop. In the 1790s it would not have needed a very practised eye to tell the difference between a melon house, a vinery, a pine house or a peach stove. Not only was there a wide range in building types but the range of crops grown in them was remarkably large. Even in the reign of George I, several sorts of melon and cucumber were commonly grown and available to the rich all the year round, but so were forced peas, lettuce and even asparagus. In the early part of the period these were produced on hot-beds rather than in greenhouses, and as the former gave rise to an important means of heating the latter, I shall discuss them first.

It was about the middle of the seventeenth century that the fermentation of horse dung or tree bark was first put to use. Both substances were extensively available. There was no competition for the dung from the stables, and only the tannery wanted some of the bark from the sawyer. Dung and bark, when kept under suitable conditions, were found to give out heat when they decomposed. Of course, other organic debris does the same, but straw and most leaves (except of the oak) give out little heat and are quickly finished; cow dung reaches too high a temperature. A well-set-up bark or dung pit would give out a good growing heat for several months, and the heat could, with some skill with the watering-can, be kept fairly constant throughout that time. The simplest pits were simply that: a trench six to eight feet across and up to five feet or so deep, filled with several feet of dung and then a thick layer of loam into which the seeds were planted. Glazed frames were then placed on top. Plants and frames were moved to another pit when the dung needed renewing. More generally the pits were only

This elegant orangery at Heveningham Hall is by Wyatt. Note the glass roof.

Orangeries were designed by the most eminent architects of the day. This example at Kenwood is by Robert Adam.

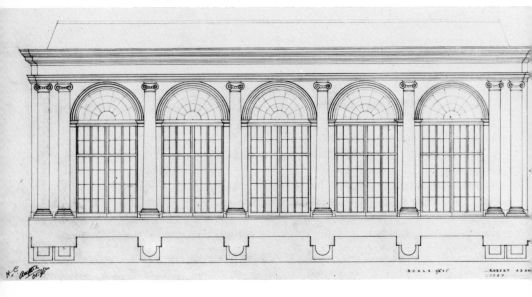

partly sunk, having brick walls back and front, the back one a foot or so higher, and with a glass sash between it and the lower one, like a modern frame. Such pits were, if possible, orientated east–west, to take full advantage of the sun. Occasionally the back wall had a chimney flue along its length, with a firebox at one end, and the chimney at the other. More rarely the flue was carried along the centre of the pit. Flued pits brought the moist bark or dung more quickly up to the correct temperature, without having to wait for natural processes to achieve the same level. The growing season was thus extended. Still more elaborate pits had rack and pinions to raise the walls and glass sashes as the plants inside grew; others were not sunk at all and had complicated mechanisms so that the spent manure could be replaced without disturbing the plants above. Conditions inside the frame were extremely humid. Often a young gardener was employed full time in wiping condensation from the glass. At night, flannel blinds were pulled over the plants to keep the drips off. After the pineapple was introduced at the beginning of the eighteenth century, pits were used extensively in the production of that fruit, and with great success. The plants rooted freely into the fermenting core of the pits and produced fruit that were said to have extraordinarily good flavour. The humble pea, sown outside in September, was moved to the pit the following month and would produce a crop for the table the next March. The only flowers that seem to have been forced in this way were the tuberose and lily-of-the-valley. The forcing pit was always located near the dung pit, not in the garden or even the kitchen garden. Any establishment that kept four or more horses had enough heat available to grow its own pineapples.

The use of orangeries has already been mentioned. Throughout the seventeenth century none had a glass roof. Stephen Switzer was the first to use this innovation, in a greenhouse for the Duke of Rutland at Belvoir. They were soon built with some magnificence. Miller wrote, in 1739, of the vast improvements in such buildings even since the first edition of the *Dictionary*, and the most splendid example then was Lord Petre's at Thorndon Hall in Essex. One of the largest was eventually built by William Chambers at Kew. The earliest were either unheated or simply had an often rather elegant open fireplace. Later ones adopted the method of heating first used in flued walls. These were really just large versions of the back wall of the pit already described. Often being the northernmost wall of the kitchen garden, and therefore with one side facing south, they had chimney flues rising slowly backwards and forwards along their length, terminating in a chimney-pot just above the coping, which was often disguised as an urn. There was one firebox for about every forty feet of wall. When a fire was lit in the stove, often with difficulty, the whole wall that it served became warm. Usually the south side was of brick and the north of stone. The brick more easily transferred the heat from the flue and so to the plants attached to the outside. Many examples are still to be seen in large kitchen gardens, although I have not seen any still in use. They were more often used at the end of the season, to prevent frost injuring new wood and to help late fruit to ripen. They were more rarely used to force trees into flower in the early spring, in which case the fires were lit during the day rather than at night. Some walls had large rollerblinds at the top, but with blinds of soft bast matting rather than fabric. These were pulled down in cold or inclement weather to protect the plants. It was only a short step to provide them first with sloping frames of oiled paper, which was transparent and waterproof and could be removed in summer, or with properly glazed frames. It was this last arrangement that proved the ancestor of the entire range of kitchen-garden glass. The orangery's only real descendants were the conservatory and perhaps the camellia house, both strongly architectural and found only in the flower garden.

Almost all kitchen glass, well into Victorian times, was attached to walls (what we now call 'lean-to'). This arrangement was surprisingly flexible, in all senses of that word, as we shall see. However, flued back walls, or floors, gave heat with certain disadvantages. Because slow-burning stoves were not available until the first few years of the nineteenth century (by which time iron-casting techniques were sufficiently sophisticated), the fire was difficult to regulate. It was difficult, too, to keep the fires actually burning all night, and impossible to cope with sudden frosts or cold spells. The quality of heat, too, left much to be desired, for it was very dry, and that encouraged many insect pests. It also did not provide a good environment for some of the more tropical crops. The obvious solution was to move the bark pit bodily into the glasshouse. The heat was steady and moist and needed little maintenance. Fire heat would be needed only in the severest weather. This combination was adopted for the whole range of glasshouses. It was less common in orangeries and conservatories, where the smell might offend the ladies.

James Shaw published *Plans of Forcing-Houses in Gardening* in 1794, which was the first general work on the topic, although a great deal had been written in earlier gardening works. By 1794, the glasshouse had reached its maximum point of diversity. He illustrated plans for forcing-walls, melon stoves (for potatoes and French beans as well), peach and nectarine stoves, vineries, pine stoves (of two sorts, one for summer fruiting, the other for winter), conservatories and greenhouses (the latter for plants needing less heat than the inhabitants of the former). The peach house had a back wall twelve to fourteen feet high, and glass sashes sloping from the top almost to ground-level. The sashes were all movable, using the same mechanism as that found in house windows. Their weight must have been enormous. The back wall was trellised, so that the branches tied to it would not touch the hot surface of the wall. Alternate dwarf and tall nectarines were planted, so that the dwarfs being against the lower and warmer part would flower and fruit earlier than the tall trees. Trees required to fruit even later than the tall trees at the back, were often trained up the glass, the low wall on which the sashes rested being on arched foundations so that the tree roots would reach the outside world. The central part of the floorspace contained a dungpit, on which Shaw suggested that strawberries, potatoes and cucumbers could be forced: a very productive arrangement.

Vineries were built largely for show. More usually the serious production of grapes and pineapples was combined in a single house, with the vines grown up the glass and so providing shade for the pineapples below. The vinery had purely decorative plants growing on the back wall, as well as on the bark or dung bed, the vines growing up wires stretched along the sash beams. There were more than twenty-five varieties of grape available for forcing, some of which have now vanished. The houses were usually cooled down once the fruit had almost ripened, and the clusters of grapes could be gathered when needed right through until the following spring (ashes were spread on the floor to dry out the air, as dampness caused rotting). If the vinery had to be kept warm for the other denizens, or if pineapples were wanted in winter, the grapes were picked, wrapped in paper and stored in tubs of bran.

The pine house (or stove) was quite similar in construction, though often split into three sections, each warmer than the last. The first was for rooting suckers and crowns. The suckers were removed from fruited plants, but the crowns, being such a decorative part of the fruit, were cut from it at the dinner-table and later returned to the gardener. In town, they were labelled and returned to the nurseryman. Rooted crowns would produce another fruit in two years. The second section of the pine house was for growth, and the third for fruiting. If, by mischance, too many fruits were coming into readiness at the same time, a proportion of them were moved to a cool shed (there were plenty of these on the north side of the wall), and this slowed them down. In the 1730s a well-built house might cost £48 and, if it was near a source of coal or bark, would cost about £5 a year to run. Such a house would produce a hundred or more fruit, requiring about three to four hundred plants at different stages. According to the variety of the pineapple, and its culture, each fruit might weigh four pounds. Gardeners, as is their wont, naturally tried to produce monstrously large fruit, although the flavour was sometimes poor. The largest one I have come across was harvested in July 1821, for Lord Cawdor at Stackpole Court, It weighed ten pounds eight ounces and was ten and a half inches in length. The price at Covent Garden for pineapples was twelve shillings a pound in the same year. Normally, pineapples were cut just before full ripeness, otherwise the flavour weakened, and they were cut with about four inches of stalk for ease of handling. A footman would hold it, while a slice was cut onto each plate. They were very commonly sent as gifts between friends and were (and remain) symbols of luxury and delight. The British Ambassador in Paris in 1817, not finding any decent fruit in the markets of that city, and with a banquet to prepare, sent the diplomatic coach all the way to London just to buy them.

With the introduction of scale insects and mealy-bugs in the early eighteenth century, a search was begun to find a means of killing them. Of course, aphids and thrips had already become a menace, but the former were at least controlled by fumigating with tobacco smoke (using a special bellows) or dusting with snuff. Thrips and red spider were removed by washing plants with soapy water or with turpentine and flowers of sulphur. Scale and mealy-bug cures were all more lethal sounding, using noxious mixtures of henbane, walnut leaves or cheap wine. One of the most lethal of all involved pounding a mixture of mercury and soft soap into a paste, diluting it and immersing plants for three hours. One hopes not too much mercury remained trapped in the scales of the fruit.

With the orangery-greenhouse and the conservatory, we leave the kitchen garden for the flower garden and the pleasure ground. Housing only ornamental plants and being usually more closely attached to the main house, both were conceived from an architectural, rather than a horticultural, point of view. Miller illustrated an excellent example.

When the orangery was superseded by the greenhouse, flue-heating took over from the open fire. Plants were usually in pots on staging, and although most plants were there all year, occasionally roses, hyacinths, pinks and carnations were forced and then taken indoors. The conservatory was kept warmer than the greenhouse, and the plants were generally bedded out and so were permanent fixtures. In the last part of the eighteenth century, the use of cast iron became commonplace and was rapidly taken up in glasshouse construction. J. C. Loudon himself invented a cast yet flexible glazing bar, the rigidity of the completed house being considerably dependent on the glass panes themselves. The fact that the bars could be bent in any direction meant that greenhouses no longer had to be rectilinear but could take on the most exotic shapes. Loudon produced many remarkable designs. To everyone's alarm, these structures waved about like large jellies before they were glazed; afterwards they froze satisfactorily. The shed-like appearance of the greenhouse vanished for the next seventy or so years. None built was as dramatic as some of Loudon's most fantastic schemes, where palaces and castles became almost totally enveloped in balloons of glass and iron. The ability to have curved roofs stilled the arguments about what angle the normal flat roof should have to the sun; a curved roof allowed at least part of itself to be always perpendicular to the sun's rays. Incidentally, Loudon allowed the patent for his bars to go to the ironfounders. He made no money from it, and it would have been one of his few really profitable ventures.

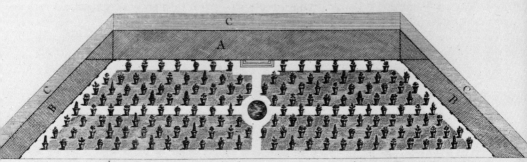

The Upright of the Greenhouse and Stoves.

A. *The Ground-plot of the Greenhouse.* B. *The Ground-plot of the Stoves.* C. *The Sheds behind the Stoves and Greenhouse.*

Above: A handsome orangery from *The Gardeners' Dictionary*, showing how the trees should be arranged in summer.

Left: A suggestion for using Loudon's curvilinear glazing bars.

Below: Steam enabled very large conservatories to be uniformly heated. This example is an interior view of the one at The Grange.

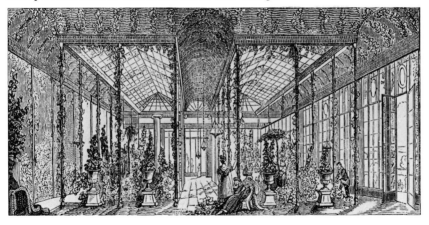

A man always full of ideas in an already inventive age, he suggested conservatories that could be dismantled during the summer, describing one at Nuneham that grew marvellous citrus trees that were planted in the open ground. A similar idea was proposed by Repton, and the framework of the house was covered with awnings during the summer and used as a tent. Loudon's main suggestion was for a 'polyprosopic' house, which provided an arrangement that was more responsive to the weather. The walls and roof were divided into pieces, hinged together rather like a Venetian blind. By opening the pieces, the plants inside could receive all the benefits of natural wind and rain as and when desired. No one took the idea up. The breakage rate of the glass panes would perhaps have been too high. As it was, generally 5 per cent of the glass needed replacing every year. By Loudon's time, good crown glass was used, and although much of it can still be seen in the windows of Georgian houses, it was very fragile. In glasshouses, the glass was only puttied at the sides where it touched a glazing bar. In winter, water accumulated in the overlap between the panes, and if it froze, the panes often broke. Early glasshouses were often glazed with cheap green glass, although opulent orangeries were glazed with the best Bohemian crystal.

Smoke heat eventually replaced tan or dung heat and was in its turn ousted by steam heat. A few attempts at steam heating had been made about 1788 but, because the pipes were poor, had not been very effective. By 1816 cast-iron techology had vastly improved (partly effected by the necessities of war), and it was then possible to make good pipes and airtight stoves. Steam proved to have many advantages and was soon used even in commercial houses. Flues and pipes were never overheated, and the heat could be carried at an even temperature for a considerable distance. Consequently a single furnace could heat several greenhouses and even the main residence itself. The cast-iron tubes were small and neat and could easily be sunk beneath the paths. The paths themselves were now formed of cast-iron gratings, usually by the firm of Bailey & Co., and were the forerunners of many still to be seen in municipal and academic greenhouses. Further, moist heat was easily obtained, and it had no smell. The modern age had begun.

Modern, too, were a multitude of ideas for fully automatic gardening. Loddiges, the great nursery in London, had a device for automatic watering, which simulated rain. There were a few private examples both in that city and in Edinburgh. Attempts were made for automatic ventilation. One wonders how effective they were. One used inflated bladders, of which one end was fixed to a movable sash and the other to a fixed bar or the wall. When the temperature rose, the air in the bladder expanded, so making it rounder and shorter. The shortening pulled open the sash and let cool air into the house. A more conventional method made use of the thermal expansion of long rods of lead.

The Georgian glasshouse shows, in some ways more than any other aspect of gardening, the immense changes that went on throughout the reign of the four kings. At the beginning of the dynasty, glasshouses, however inelegant, were owned only by the wealthy and could provide conditions for only a limited number of species. By the death of George IV, glasshouses were being virtually mass-produced, built and heated by completely new technologies. They could provide correct conditions for plants of almost any habitat, from the lushest jungle to the most Alpine cliff, and could certainly cope with the immense influx of plants, brought from every continent in the world by traders, explorers and scientists, the most important men of the new century.

17. Kitchen gardens

The kitchen garden was, in almost every way, the most conservative part of the Georgian garden and can be traced back in a substantially similar form for many centuries. Certainly, an example from the reign of George I would have looked very little different from any during the reign of George IV; perhaps the glasshouses in the latter would have been larger and less cumbersome. In contrast to the pleasure garden and the grounds, fashion and conspicuous expenditure played little part. The pleasures of productivity were all. Also in comparison with the decorative garden, only a small number of new crop types were introduced during the period, tomatoes and Brussels sprouts being perhaps the most notable, although potatoes only now became really well and widely used, and the cauliflower became more popularly eaten. Before examining the range of produce available (which would have put any modern greengrocer or fruiterer to shame), it is important to examine the basic form of the garden and the way in which it was related to the needs and status of the owner.

Every kitchen garden of any size was walled, at least on three sides, with walls up to sixteen feet high. Almost all were rectangular, although there are rare examples of trapezoid and oval ones. Most were square, with the sides facing each arm of the compass. All the inner wall space was utilized for espalier fruit trees or for vines, and in many cases the outer walls too. If this was the case, the garden was often protected from marauders by a ha-ha or fence, a broad ditch or even a moat. To protect the garden from winds (from their cooling powers; nothing could protect the garden from gale damage), it was surrounded at a distance of sixty feet by thick plantations, often of hollies, yews or beeches. The area between the walls and the plantation was called the 'slip' and was either grassed or devoted to informally planted orchards or soft fruit such as black and red currants. where the garden was small enough to need only one entrance, it was in the middle of the south wall. This was the least useful one horticulturally, and the visitor, entering through it, was confronted immediately with a view of the highly productive wall to the north, often with glasshouses and sometimes broken in the middle by the façade of the head gardener's house. Every garden had two main paths, north–south and west–east, bordered in small gardens by parsley or strawberries, in large ones by rows of espaliered trees (usually apples) attached to a wooden latticework painted dark green or deep red. Many examples still exist, some with the original trees, now gnarled but often still productive. The largest walled gardens and most Scottish ones, whatever the size, also enclosed the flower garden, and the division between them was marked by a cross-wall (sometimes waved in plan and called 'crinkum-crankum') or a terrace. In the flower garden, the cruciform arrangement of the paths was usually repeated.

The north wall, often flued from the 1730s, supported on its south side all the main fruits, but especially plums, peaches and nectarines. On its north face were potting sheds, gardeners' quarters and storage sheds. Some walls were buttressed or even niched, to provide sheltered conditions for grapes. Where there were no vineries, these were commonly grown in the open, and with considerable success, the Duke of Norfolk producing his own burgundy from open-grown vines. Grapes that were not ripe by the end of the season were pressed to provide verjuice and used in cooking. The side walls of the garden supported fruit that needed less heat and light to ripen their fruit, particularly apples and cherries. The north side of the south wall was planted with morellos behind, currants and gooseberries in front, and in front of those were beds for cuttings and young plants of all kinds. A rotation was carried out between the four quarters of the garden. Leguminous crops were in one part, various root crops in the two others, and the last was either fallow or in grass (if the latter, it was used as the drying green for the main house).

A well-managed kitchen garden of an acre in extent, if it contained hot-beds, would employ one full-time gardener and some occasional help. It would supply fresh vegetables throughout the year, and fresh fruit for most of it, for a family of four, but would provide nothing for the servants. A garden of this size was considered suitable for members of the minor gentry or for the wealthier farmers. The normal farmer's kitchen garden would enclose only about one quarter of an acre which, apart from staple vegetables, would probably have supplied broccoli, artichokes, spinach, fennel and asparagus. The main fruits in it would have been apples, plums and cherries. In such modest establishments the white Dutch currant would take the place of grapes and be used both fresh and to make wine. The wine was very popular and could be bought for a shilling a bottle; it was often diluted with water to make a cooling drink in summer. The richest gentry, with a kitchen garden of about five acres, would have hot walls for peaches and nectarines, pits or glasshouses for melons and pineapples. Such a garden would cost, by 1800, £400 a year to run, which would include about £30 for

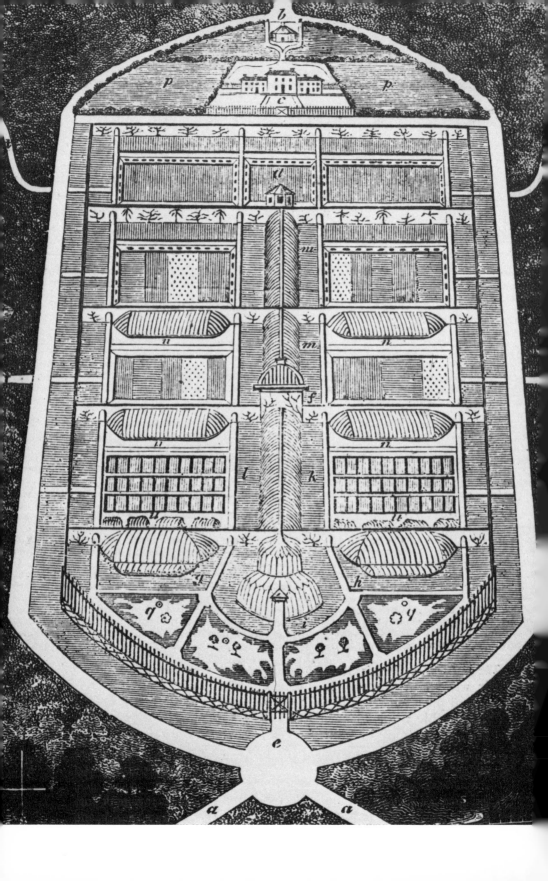

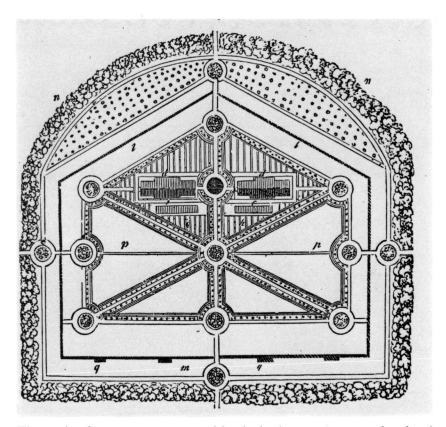

The passion for symmetry suppressed by the landscape movement often found expression in the design of the kitchen garden.

Left: A suggestion from the *Encyclopaedia of Gardening* for an elaborate kitchen garden with a number of cross-walls for fruit and glass. There is an elegant gardener's house.

seeds, tools, pots and the rest, £85 for the head gardener, and the remainder split between casual labour and coal for heating. Most noblemen had gardens up to eight acres in extent, but the grandest gardens were far larger. The most princely one in Scotland was owned by the Dukes of Buccleuch at Dalkeith Palace. Of thirteen acres, it produced cherries and cucumbers all through the year, had two vineries fifty feet long, a stove house of forty feet, and four hundred feet of melon frames. It is still in use as a market garden. English examples are quite as grand, and most ducal houses would have had something comparable.

Some of the vegetables grown have already been mentioned. Many are scarcely used today, although some (fennel, salsify and celeriac) are coming back into notice. Today, of course, it is so easy to import, and to store, the commoner sorts that the unusual ones have become rarer as they often require more skill to cook. Fennel was then used not as salad but as a sauce for mackerel, or put under the loaves in an oven to flavour the bread. Artichoke hearts were fried in batter or added, fresh or pickled, to fish and meat stews. Asparagus was well known. It was also very large, for there were commonly only six shoots to the pound (in Holland there were only three). Sea kale was thought by many to have a better flavour. Other substitutes for asparagus were the young shoots of the hop plant and the young flowering stems of the scorzonera, more usually grown for its roots. The stems really are quite as good as asparagus. Cardoons were very widely grown, as was celeriac, both often eaten raw or cold after cooking, with oil and vinegar. Sorrel, only on fashionable tables, was used boiled as a sauce for veal or pork, or instead of apple sauce on wild goose. The range of greens used as salads was enormous, encompassing many things we now think of as weeds. The dandelion was blanched and eaten, and the shepherd's purse was actively encouraged. It is still used as a salad in the Orient. Scurvy grass, samphire, burnet (also added to wine to alleviate the after-effects), even the rampion (*Campanula rapunculus*, its roots eaten like radishes) and the wood sorrel were common ingredients. The tomato, then more usually called the 'love-apple', became common only at the beginning of the nineteenth century and was used in soups and sauces, in ketchups (then taken with mutton) or as a preserve or pickled. It was believed to be an aphrodisiac, as was the aubergine. Only the white-skinned variety of this was available, which is now rarely seen and not eaten with any high hopes. Late Georgian, too, was the Brussels sprout. They were first marketed in Britain still attached to the main stalk, although eaten as in Brussels, with oil, vinegar and nutmeg. While many vegetables were available fresh throughout the year, a few sorts were stored. Cabbages, carrots, endives, even chicory and lettuce were boxed in dry sand and placed in a cool cellar.

Herbs were widely grown, although, with the increasing popularity of French cuisine throughout the period, food became less highly flavoured.

Some surprising plants were used in cooking. Marigold petals were used in soups and broths to give them a good colour. Clary was used in the same way, adding flavour as well, and was also used in clary wine. Tansy gave colour and flavour to cakes and puddings, as well as being used in the embalming of corpses. There was no diminution in their use as simple medicinal remedies, for many herbs were used for curing everything from worms and tuberculosis to syphilis. Even the humble rhubarb (of which three species were commonly grown and eaten) was thought to be useful for the latter.

Of the soft fruits, and here should be included pumpkins (then called 'pompions' and often baked stuffed with apples and spices, or fried in butter) as well as melons, the various berries were widely grown and used so flexibly as to put the modern cook to shame. Mulberries, now rare, were common at dessert or were turned into wine. The unripe berries were put into a syrup used as a gargle in throat infections, and the tree bark was used as a vermifuge. Several species of *Berberis* had their fruits candied and were used as a garnish on roast game and as a sauce for hare, as well as for sweet puddings. Elderberries were used in a highly valued wine, and the flowers, dried and put into muslin sachets, were used to flavour custards, puddings and wine, and even to make an expectorant. Gooseberries were used as now; wine made from them was quite as popular in middle-class families as grape wine. Many early horticultural societies gave prizes for the best gooseberry wine. Unripe fruits were picked and stored in barrels of water and later used as a tart sauce for poultry, especially goose and turkey. Black and red currants were rarely eaten fresh but were made into jellies, wines, puddings and fillings for tarts. Raspberries were used in much the same way, although eaten fresh as well, and the syrup was used to remove tartar from the teeth and also (at the same time?) as a cure for rheumatism and gout. Strawberries were eaten fresh. Several species were introduced during the eighteenth century, and by its end there were four in common cultivation. There were no fat and flavourless hybrids.

Of tree fruits, apples, pears, plums and cherries had been grown from very early times. Even when George I came to the throne, there was a very large number of variety names for each species, but no one knew how many distinct types really existed. The situation became worse, for from the mid-century a great deal of deliberate breeding was carried out, in both Britain and Europe. The number of varieties expanded alarmingly, and names became so confused that the only way to buy fruit trees was to sample fruit at the nursery and place an order based on that. By the end of the century, the major London nurseries had almost two hundred and fifty sorts of apple for sale, more than one hundred and fifty pears, forty plums and the same number of cherries. For the sorts of fruit that had to be kept, fruit rooms were attached to the north wall of the kitchen garden or in small establishments in the attics of the principal residence. Very grand houses sometimes had storage rooms built below ground next to the ice-house (a necessary item for the luxurious), so that fruit could be kept at low temperatures. Thus, there was almost no time of year without fresh fruit. Of fruits that would not store, cherries were placed in brandy, candied or turned into wine. The quince, which would store well if need be, could be turned into marmalade or, if used fresh, was combined with apples in pies. Excess peaches were preserved, chutnied or used to flavour brandy. Nectarines and apricots were used in the same way (the leaves and young shoots were used to make a dye). Medlars were eaten in November, just as they began to decay, by those who had that sort of taste. Nuts were widely grown. Only the chestnut and sometimes the walnut were used as part of the 'architecture' of the wider garden. Almonds and filberts were kept to the 'slips'. Brazil nuts, cashews and pecans were imported, although sometimes grown in the conservatory. I doubt if they ever yielded a crop.

Pests and diseases were the same as those of today. To deter, or catch, the largest predator, most nurserymen carried an extensive range of man-traps. For lesser animals soapy water, snuff or tobacco was sufficient. Labour was cheap, and so caterpillars were usually gathered by hand, trees being brushed with besoms beforehand or sprayed with hot water. There were many types of bird-scarer, from the traditional scarecrow to the more amusing mock cats, herons and eagles. Windmills, black thread or thread tied with feathers were all hopeful additions, but, then as now, nets and real men were always more effective. What we now know to be a fungal disease, finger-and-toe, was attributed to a mysterious insect resident in old gardens. The only cure ever suggested was to dip brassica seedling roots in soap-ash mud or in soot. I should not think either worked. Of the other diseases, too little of their nature was understood, and few cures were suggested. It may have been that diseases were less important then, for breeding pressures for disease resistance, or at least tolerance, were much stronger than today, when the availability of so many fungicides means that new varieties can be selected for yield rather than any other quality.

18. Gardeners

In 1778 John Abercrombie published *Every Man his own Gardener*. Himself a reasonably successful gardener, born, as many were, in Scotland and having worked at Kew and become head gardener at Leicester House, he yet felt that his own name was insufficient 'pull' for the sale of his book. He arranged to pay the head gardener of the Duke of Leeds £20 for the use of his better-known name. The book was an immediate success and was still selling well long after Abercrombie's death in 1806. However, after its first appearance, Abercrombie felt that he ought to meet Mr Mawe (the Duke of Leeds's gardener) and give him his thanks. He arrived at the garden and at once saw a gentleman powdered and splendidly dressed. He bowed deeply, thinking him to be the Duke himself. It was, in fact, the head gardener.

Of course, not all head gardeners lived as comfortably as those attached to great estates. Some prospered, as did Abercrombie, more through print than planting. Others appear only in the prize lists of the various horticultural societies; thousands are forgotten. Very little at all is known of the immense numbers of apprentices, journeymen and jobbers, or of the itinerant boys, children and old women employed to pick caterpillars from the vegetables. Only towards the end of the period, with its growing interest in the plight of such deprived classes, do we hear much of the living conditions of the humbler denizens of the garden. In the 1820s, for instance, watering-boys for the more important greenhouses were paid a maximum of eight shillings a week. Apprentices got only a shilling or so more. The men all boarded together, usually in the lean-to sheds on the north side of the kitchen garden, often sleeping two or three in a bed and with their meals cooked either by themselves or by an old female servant paid even less than they. They had to start work by six in the morning or earlier (at Fonthill they had to scythe the lawns at night), and the garden work was finished twelve hours later. In the better-run gardens, they then had to study gardening, botany and various other sciences until nine at night. They were fined for leaving implements dirty, for absence, for not having with them a knife or apron, and even for not knowing the Latin name for plants in the garden. Like children, they were often allowed small pieces of ground for their own cultivation. The head gardener gave prizes for the best patch. Organized in various departments (glass, shrubbery, lawn, forest, etc.), they were closely supervised by foremen, whose wages were about four shillings a week more. It was they who kept the time sheets and all the departmental accounts.

An apprenticeship finished in about three years, and the new 'journeyman' could either become a jobbing gardener (in which case he had to purchase his own set of tools, and the full kit might cost the immense sum of seven or eight pounds) or remain in service. In either case, he could expect a wage of about three shillings a day, which was just sufficient, if he was self-employed and had no other income, to keep a wife and one child. A gardener with one of the London nurseries, a young Irishman, was summoned before the Marylebone magistrate and ordered to pay three shillings a week to the mother of his illegitimate child. This, he claimed, probably truthfully, would ruin him, for he was paid only ten.

Of course, London was a magnet for all indigent or ambitious journeymen, for, with its rapidly growing suburbs, jobbing gardeners were in great demand. London, too, had large nursery gardens, with a correspondingly large need for labour. However, such was the influx of gardeners that wages remained extremely low. Even bricklayers were said to earn between five and seven shillings a day, and for that they needed virtually no education. A number of indignant gardeners wrote to the *Gardeners' Magazine*, but it was pointed out to the objectors that a bricklayer had little chance of preferment, whereas it was relatively easy for the journeyman gardener to become a master gardener and therefore eligible for a head gardener's post with, in the first instance, a minor gentleman.

By that time the gardener may have joined one of the gardeners' lodges. These, organized along Masonic lines, were a cross between a benevolent organization and a professional society but were falling into disuse by the 1820s. The oldest had been founded in Aberdeen, and was called 'Adam's Lodge'. A London branch had been opened in 1781. Banff had 'Solomon's Lodge', and Edinburgh had the 'Caledonian', founded in 1790. For some reason, perhaps the quality of his early education or a national touch of ambition, almost every master gardener in England and many head gardeners on the Continent (and even in Russia) were Scots. Even Scots jobbing gardeners were much sought after, and no doubt some of this was due to the influence of the lodges. By the beginning of the nineteenth century, the lodges were falling into decline. In any case, any gardener brought up in a garden run along lines suggested by Loudon (a Scot) in the *Encyclopaedia* would have been an educated man. He wrote: "The grand drawback to every kind of improvement is the vulgar and degrading idea that certain things are beyond our reach." The suggested contents for a gardener's course included geology, chemistry, meteorology, physics and botany, and he insisted that every head gardener should have an ample library. This was not enough, and he hoped that the house-servants would teach the apprentices dancing, fencing, boxing and even backgammon, chess and the flute, saying, "To a man who has no other resources for advancement in life than such as are personal, every exterior requirement is of the utmost importance." He went on to suggest the learning of several languages and the regulation of almost everything else, including the bowels.

For those men who could not make the transition to the post of head gardener, destitution and sometimes even brutality was always fearfully close. In some northern towns, prosperous nurserymen kept their workforce, forcibly, in conditions no better than slavery. But for those that could make the change, though still hard-worked, life was rosier. The head gardener was sometimes lodged in the housekeeper's quarters, but in a garden of any size or pretension he usually had his own house. Sometimes this was one of the lodges, in which case it became his duty to show visitors round the house and grounds (often a handsomely tipped task). More often it was attached to the kitchen garden, even forming part of the architectural design. Most such houses were just large enough to accommodate a wife, two children and sometimes a single servant. The *Encyclopaedia* suggests the following minimum: a ground floor with back kitchen, front kitchen and parlour, and the upper storey with two bedrooms with cupboards. The house fixtures were to be provided by the landlord and included a water-pump, furnace and boiler for laundry and bath-water in the back kitchen, and a range, oven, dressers, tables and shelves in the front kitchen. The specifications may have been somewhat hopeful, for Loudon reports it as a common occurrence for the head gardener and his family to be lodged in the same dank sheds as the rest of the garden staff. However, many examples remain of houses in which happy and healthy lives were clearly possible, perhaps sometimes more so than in the chilly and damp attic and basement rooms in the main house.

The head gardener's job embraced a very wide range of tasks. He had to ensure a continuous supply of comestibles for the kitchens, of flowers and plants for the house, and nosegays for the ladies. As well as seeing that the gardens and greenhouses were kept in trim, he also supervised constructional work, had to introduce as many new plants as possible, had to supervise the storage of roots, fruit and seeds, and to manage the sale of excess produce. Together with all this, he had to educate his apprentices, guide visitors, sometimes even act as night-watchman. It is no wonder that many felt underpaid. Those who worked in a medium-sized garden received about £40 a year, with about eleven shillings a week 'board money'. In contrast to the butler's position, there were no other perquisites, and yet the

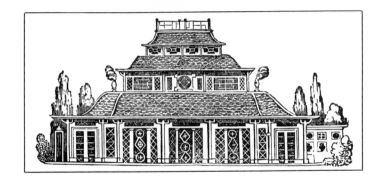

Illustrations from Loudon's *Encyclopaedia of Gardening*, showing designs for 'the dwelling of an upper servant' and (bottom) a mansion and its various-styled outbuildings.

gardener might handle wages and contracts of £3,000 or more a year. Butlers, who did not handle accounts, were generally paid £10 more a year, as well as getting two or three suits of clothes a year and a greatcoat every second one. Further, and this rankled most, however much a gardener improved himself and the staff, it was rare for the employer to increase his wages. The gardener usually had to apply for another position if he wanted to better his purse. Contracts were on a yearly basis, and references were essential. Even for the best gardener, a bad employer could ruin his career. For those who avoided disaster and who managed to save some of their salary every year, it was possible for them to buy an annuity at the age of fifty and retire on an income of eighty to a hundred pounds a year. (The stable interest rate was about 4 per cent.) If fifty now seems an early retirement age, actuarial calculations were based on death at sixty-eight (or two years less in London). How the lower garden staff kept themselves in age and infirmity is not known.

The head gardener, especially if employed by some great peer, was at the top of his profession. The only means of further advancement was to go into business and open a nursery garden, to take to print or to ascend to the realms of design. Nurseries were attached to every great city, but only the largest and most progressive (or aggressive) concerns afforded their owners even a genteel existence. The most famous nurseries were usually dependent on one strong and dynamic personality, and, when that was removed, faded away. The big ones, at their zenith, could finance collecting trips to distant lands and materially advance the science of botany. The most famous of all was Loddiges, already mentioned several times, founded by the gardener of Sir John Sylvester. The small ones, on a few acres of annually rented land, supplied poorly grown plants and cheap Dutch seed to an ignorant market.

Master gardeners who found time to write are, of course, better documented than their silent brothers. Not all of the writer-gardeners were particularly original; some were quite dishonest: the Duke of Kingston's gardener wrote *The New Gardener's Dictionary* in 1771, which was lifted almost entirely, illustrations and all, from *Eden, or a Complete Body of Gardening* by Sir John Hill. Hill, botanist, rather than gardener, to the Duke of Richmond, was none too scrupulous himself, so perhaps he did not mind. A proprietor of a quack medicine, he also wrote farces, novels and a number of vicious pamphlets. By all this, he lived well, earning more than a thousand pounds a year. *Eden* was also the quarry for a number of other writers. More worthy, if less fun, were gardeners such as William Speechley, who published works on the pineapple and on vines, Abercrombie (who also dabbled profitably in garden design) and many others.

Almost certainly the most influential of all was Philip Miller, who really merits a full chapter. Born in 1692, son of a Scots gardener, he was at first a florist, then gardener to the Company of Apothecaries and became immensely knowledgeable. There were sixteen editions of his *Dictionary*, the last appearing long after his death in 1771. It was edited by Professor Martyn and was in two vast volumes. Like many much less important men, he was consulted about design matters, even although the *Dictionary* is often rather conservative. Nevertheless, he had as patrons the Dukes of Bedford, Northumberland (Miller was consulted about the layout at Syon) and Richmond. One of his many famous pupils was William Aiton, who became head gardener at Kew and Kensington and published an immensely useful book on the plants at Kew, their place of origin and date of introduction.

Another gardener whose writings were of immense influence throughout the succeeding century was John Claudius Loudon. He, much less of a botanist, was a very prolific writer and produced not a dictionary but the immense *Encyclopaedia of Gardening* from which much has already been quoted. First appearing in 1822, it embraced every aspect of gardening, from its earliest history to the most modern methods and taste in design. Loudon's career extended well into the nineteenth century (he died in 1843), and so his greatest influence was on Victorian, rather than Georgian, gardens. However, many of his ideas were so advanced that often things that are now associated with the Victorian Age were originated by him in the previous one. Loudon was often consulted about garden design. It was perhaps his republican sympathies that led him to pay more attention to the design of lower- and middle-class housing than to upper-class gardens, and it was in the former field that his most enduring contribution was made. He was born the son of a farmer, and his first job was with a landscape gardener in Edinburgh. He moved to London in 1803 and seemed to have had no difficulty finding garden commissions. Had he restricted himself to that activity, he might have lived more easily. His ventures into print, though voluminous, were perilously expensive to produce, and he died in considerable financial difficulties. His larger works were written by an editorial team, and he commissioned articles and illustrations in great profusion. The fees and wages had to be paid before there was any income from the work in progress, and as the financial balancing act from the previous work sometimes failed, he had to keep up a continual production of new works to keep money coming in. Nevertheless, while we can feel for his private difficulties, the main books give an astonishingly vivid picture of agriculture and gardening in the early nineteenth century, for which we cannot but be grateful.

Gardeners who turned their hand to design or the written word, faced competition from men of other backgrounds. Painters, minor gentlemen, doctors and pharmacists, all took up theodolite, pen or both in the cause of garden design. One of the few painters was Alexander Nasmyth, although he was an engineer and a designer in a much wider field. Among much else,

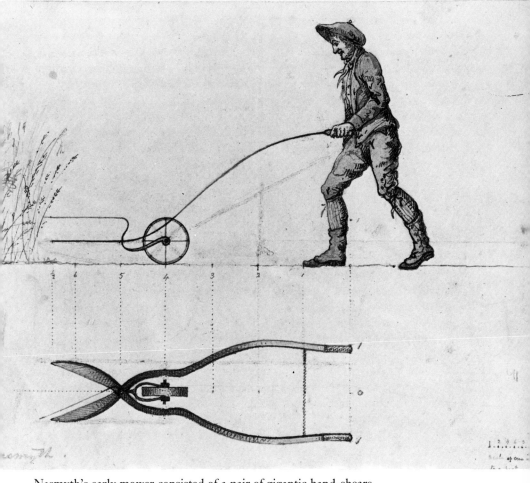

Nasmyth's early mower consisted of a pair of gigantic hand-shears.

An under gardener from Loudon's *Encyclopaedia of Gardening*.

he designed a splendid and rather dangerous-looking machine for cutting grass. In landscaping, he provided the only instance of a designer using the present-day technique of building a scale model of the landscape, complete with tiny trees and mirror for the water. Everyone else used maps and drawings. Minor gentlemen were more common as landscape practitioners. One who made a considerable impact, although his book is now quite rare, was Thomas Whately, of Nonsuch Park. His *Observations on Modern Gardening . . . illustrated by descriptions* appeared in 1770, rapidly went through several editions and was soon translated into French and German. Nonsuch (the now vanished Elizabethan prodigy house) had one of the most magnificent of any English formal gardens; it was landscaped by Whately, whom Loudon thought "the first and best of all writers on the modern style". Loudon modelled a good deal of the *Encyclopaedia* on Whately's book, as did another gentleman who has already been quoted several times on these pages, William Marshall. Marshall was born in Yorkshire and became a planter in the West Indies. He did not actually lose money, but, after various false starts, he began writing and landscaping, wintering in London and travelling to gardens during the summer. He was successful enough to purchase a large estate in the Vale of Cleveland. Walter Nicol, also already quoted, designed too and charged a guinea a day expenses and his travel expenses by horse and stage.

One man who had no need to earn money by writing was T. A. Knight. Scarcely a minor gentleman, he eventually inherited Dowton Castle (an opulent and entirely unfrivolous gothic house with sumptuous Roman interiors) from his brother Richard who took part in 'the Picturesque' debate. Thomas had none of his brother's obsessive interest in classical civilization (and erotica) and instead spent his time writing on horticulture and breeding new strawberries. He was responsible for 116 publications.

19. Books and magazines

New gardening books appeared in almost every year throughout the period; Loudon lists twenty-four published in the twenty years from 1730 to 1750, sixty-six in those from 1765 to 1785, and eighty-seven between 1800 and 1820. The trend was to continue. The numbers do not seem large by today's output, but it should be remembered that new books then, if at all successful, had a very long lifetime, appearing in many new editions. Not all of these were as themselves, for some were re-titled, some were pirated, and others were plagiarized with varying degrees of disguise. The increase in numbers of books published was related to the widening of interest in gardening and to the diversification of gardening itself, as well as to the improvements in technology that reduced the cost of printing. Authors and publishers were quick to cater for the new markets at all social levels. While books written specifically for middle-class and suburban gardeners appeared only in the last decades of the period, in the earlier part most books had been aimed either high or low. Miller did both, for he became worried that the high cost of the full-sized *Dictionary* would keep it out of the hands of the poorer gardeners, and they were often the ones whose gardens could most benefit from improvement. He issued an abridged version in a smaller format.

Some forms of book not seen today were very popular, although their modern equivalent can be found in a number of periodicals. The gardeners' 'calendar' was a very common mode of presenting garden information, and they were produced in very large numbers. Rarely large and rarely with many illustrations, they were designed for the less wealthy section of the market. All of them were split into twelve monthly sections, each detailing what work should be done in each department of the garden, whether glass, flowers, vegetables, sometimes forest and so on. While useful for the practical gardener who did not have time or inclination to read very often, calendars were often repetitive and, because of their segmental nature, were unable to expound any coherent attitude to the aesthetics or science of gardening. Few were indexed, and any specific piece of information was difficult to find. Some of the more amusing combined a gardeners' calendar with general household hints, sections on cooking and even how to hunt for what was to be cooked.

For the top end of the market some magnificently lavish books were produced. Expensive then, many fetch vast sums at present-day auctions. A number were so lavish that they ruined both author and publisher. Few made a great deal of money. The expense, then as now, was usually based on the quality of the illustration. One of the first to appear after 1730 was Robert Furber's *Twelve Months of Flowers* in 1732. It cost the substantial sum of £2.14s.6d. if the plates were coloured, less if they were plain. It was basically a catalogue, Furber being a nurseryman, and so each of the flowers illustrated was numbered so that patrons could order their own plants. The plates are of marvellous artistic and botanical quality. The end of the century and the beginning of the next saw numerous lush examples, many masquerading as botanical monographs. Some have already been mentioned. Thornton wrote of his *Temple of Flora*, which was quite magnificent:

> Each scenery [behind the plants illustrated] is appropriate to the subject. Thus in the night-blowing Cereus you have the moon playing on the dimpled water, and the turret-clock points to XII, the hour at night when this flower is at its full expanse [he does not explain what a clock-tower or a lake is doing in the middle of the desert]. In the large-flowering Mimosa, first discovered in the mountains of Jamaica, you have the humming-birds of that country, and one of the aborigines struck with the peculiarities of the plant. . . .

All very fine, but the expense of producing the plates proved so much that Thornton had to persuade Parliament to let him hold a public lottery to keep him solvent. The prize was the set of original paintings for the plates.

One of the most famous colour-plated works, and one with only moderate ambitions, still appears today. This was, and is, the *Botanical Magazine*. When it started up in 1787, it was realized that if such expensive plates were to reach a wide audience, the best way to do this would be to release them as part-works spread over a number of years, or indefinitely. (There had been earlier examples: Miller's illustrations had reached the subscribers between 1755 and 1760, and William Hanbury's *Complete Body of Planting and Gardening. . .*, begun in 1769, was completed in 150 sixpenny weekly parts which formed two handsome volumes.) The '*Bot. Mag.*' as it is known to most botanists, started up under the direction of an ex-apothecary turned botanist called William Curtis. It appeared irregularly at first, then became popular. It almost vanished after the death of its owner in 1799 but was bought up by some of his relations in 1827 and still flourishes. Its successful formula was attempted by many others. The nursery of Loddiges started up the *Botanical Cabinet* in 1817, following the format of the *Botanical Register*

A midsummer plate from Furber's *Twelve Months of Flowers* of 1732. All the plants could be ordered from his nursery.

of 1815. The latter confined itself only to exotic plants and had often superb plates. There were many others. Morris's *Flora Conspicua* cost three shillings and sixpence per part. Robert Sweet, a bookseller, virtually specialized in the production of part-works. Some were worthily scientific (for example, *The Geraniaceae* from 1820), but most were frankly popular (*The British Flower Garden* from 1822, and *The Florist's Guide and Cultivator's Directory* from 1827).

Gardening magazines also began during the same period. The first was published by the energetic J. C. Loudon. It began in 1826, appearing haphazardly, but by the end of the decade was appearing bi-monthly, alternating with the *Magazine of Natural History* edited by the same man. It was cheap, aimed largely at the gardener in service and profusely illustrated by woodcuts of excellent quality. It projected its editor's views very strongly; liberal, even republican, it encouraged the oppressed to free themselves through education rather than revolution, although fully in sympathy with the recent events in France. It also advocated some urban planning schemes which borrowed much from the wilder visions of the French neo-classical architects. Moderately successful until the launch, in 1831, of a competitor edited by Paxton, it was then forced into a slow decline. It gives a marvellous picture of late-Georgian gardens for, among articles on pest control, book reviews (on architecture, as well as the hundreds of travel and geography books), articles on growing rare plants and the plight of the agricultural poor, is a splendid series entitled "Calls at Suburban gardens". The suburbs were defined geographically rather than socially, for volume two included a visit to Buckingham House, the garden of which received some very caustic and anti-Hanoverian comment. An almost incendiary article about the extravagant iniquities of the Duke of Chandos's palace at Canons (the house had been stripped and demolished in the previous century, giving rise to a fascinating sale catalogue) appeared in the same volume. So did an article on Whitmore Lodge, which described the house interiors with, curiously, a sycophancy worthy of some of today's decorators' magazines.

The fusion of horticultural and architectural interests was largely a preoccupation of the period from 1790. From that time there were numerous examples of books of villa and cottage design, each usually showing elevations of the buildings set in garden-landscapes judged suitable to the house style and social position. Authors ranged from the eminent John Soane to very minor figures for whom the books were largely hopeful self-advertisements. J. B. Papworth's fine publications have generally more garden than architecture, but the gardens were really settings for the architectural elements already described, as well as some amusing houses. The plates show gardens very much in the fashion of the early nineteenth century and very similar to the later works of Repton. Of course, books

Books with plates like these were eagerly bought and played a large part in educating the public taste. These examples are from Neale's *Views of the Seats of Noblemen and Gentlemen* of 1824. *Above:* Fyvie Castle. *Below:* Bury Hill, Surrey.

solely on garden buildings had been published throughout the eighteenth century, starting off with Batty Langley's early architectural works but becoming especially popular in the 1750s, a decade boasting William Halfpenny's *New Designs for Chinese Temples* of 1752, Charles Over's overwhelmingly titled *Ornamental Architecture in the Gothic, Chinese and Modern Taste, being over fifty intire [sic] new Designs (Many of which may be Executed with the Roots of Trees), for Gardens, Parks, Forests, Woods, Canals, etc.* of 1758, and Paul Decker's *Gothick Architecture; garden buildings, etc.* of 1759.

Although only indirectly concerned with the story of gardening, travel books were produced in very large numbers in the early nineteenth century. Many of these described parts of the growing empire, but travel within Britain itself became much easier as the road system improved from the end of the eighteenth century onwards. Much of the island (once almost as foreign as America or India) became easily visited. Enterprising men saw the possibilities in combining topography, architecture and gardening, together with a good dash of snobbery.

The field had been opened much earlier with Jan Kip's *Britannia Illustrata* of 1709. This work shows aerial views of so many superb early houses and gardens that one can only mourn the number of terrible losses. Thomas Badeslade's *Thirty-six views of Noblemen's and Gentlemen's Seats* is a rather similar work of 1720. There was then a long gap, while the taste changed and the new style consolidated. Indeed, there was time for the new gardens to mature, for Watt's *Seats of the Nobility and Gentry*, which was a part-work, did not begin to appear until 1779. The most important, because it was profusely illustrated and covered so much of the country, although not giving a great deal of information about the gardens, was John Neale's *Views of the Seats of Noblemen and Gentlemen* of 1824. The illustrations may often be found as separate prints.

While this sort of publication was undoubtedly important in forming the public taste, 'the Picturesque' movement was based on more truly topographical works, most of which have been discussed. However, for the very many amateur artists of the day, and especially for those who wanted to make picturesque or Gilpinesque watercolours, a number of publications were devoted to the ancillary details necessary for the style but not always available in the real landscape. Designs were given groups of ragged peasants, shaggy livestock of all kinds, ruins, decaying cottages, gipsies, bandits and other dangerous inhabitants rarely to be found in the Home Counties.

All these books, from didactic doggerel about landscape design to near-botanical treatises on garden flowers, helped gardeners who could not themselves visit the most new, chaste and elegant examples of the latest in garden design. For those who could, a number of guide-books were produced, especially for the most visited garden of all: Stowe. Visitors were then much more interested in design and planting than many seem to be today. Other books, especially Whately's *Observations* and Marshall's *Planting and Rural Ornament*, gave detailed descriptions of several gardens, notably The Leasowes, Fisherwick, Piercefield and Enville. Not unexpectedly, the most detailed list of all is found in Loudon's *Encyclopaedia*. Many gardens admired and visited in the early nineteenth century still exist, and the more important ones can be found in the final section of this book.

20. *The final elements*

Before going on to the gardens themselves, there are a few last aspects of gardening that form some very important elements in the landscape garden which have not yet found a place in these pages: lawns, water, walks and boundaries.

Lawns, of course, had been essential in the earlier formal gardens, either in the parterre as a foil to the elaborate box and flower work (and called a *plat anglais* in France) or in the deer park with its web of great avenues. In the gardens of the eighteenth century, however, the lawns of the garden were meant to be walked on, ridden over or picnicked on. Those of the park were to act as foils not to box edgings but to noble forests and lakes and to the house itself. Britain's climate is ideally suited to the production of grass, and even in the seventeenth century lawns were thought of as the essence of English gardening. In the eighteenth they were, certainly near the house, most carefully made. The greatest attention was paid to drainage and soil quality. If they were to be seeded, ready-made mixtures of six or seven grass species were easily procured and were usually mixed with 10 per cent of clover seed. The clover provided nitrogen for the grasses. No chemical fertilizer was yet in use, and the lawns near the house were not grazed and so not dunged. As there were no weedkillers but the gardeners, the modern obsession with weed-free lawns had no place in garden thinking. Indeed, the subtle changes in colour and texture that the weeds provided were appreciated.

There were no lawn mowers either, and although various inventions had been tried, including fearsome contraptions similar to the one designed by Nasmyth already illustrated, none had been a success. All lawns were scythed and then rolled. This was so even at the end of the period, J. B. Papworth commenting on the considerable nuisance to the more fortunate members of a country household: "The lawn is in general very much restricted in point of size, for the labour that is imagined to be necessary to keep it mown, but this is a great error, which perhaps proceeds from the silly habit that the mower has of indicating his industry by the frequent use of the gritstone in sharpening his scythe, and generally at the time of morning that such noises are most tormenting." (The lawns of the squares in London were cut only once a fortnight, even in summer.) The grass was not cut until quite long, for otherwise the blade could not do its work. Scything always left a slightly irregular surface, however carefully the grass was rolled afterwards. Georgian lawns now cut with modern machinery have a dapper smoothness that they would not originally have had. When the present sort of elegance was wanted, perhaps sometimes in the flower garden, hand-shears were used. At least one garden-owner was very much aware of these differences in surface texture and in 1829 left very specific instructions to his descendants that on no account were shears to be used on any part of the lawn. That particular lawn has vanished beneath scrub and fallen masonry. Garden-rollers have scarcely changed in design, although in the eighteenth century rollers for large lawns were pulled by a horse, whose hooves were covered with large padded overshoes to stop hoof-prints on the lawn. Perhaps the same horse was fed the hay.

The further lawn, separated from the garden one by a ha-ha, a sunk fence or an elegant iron railing, was grazed. While on small estates the livestock was most likely to be cows or, more rarely, sheep, ancient families or great landowners usually grazed deer. Many of the paintings in Repton's Red Books show deer resting beneath a clump of oaks as a foreground for the view. In some cases this would have been a subtle sort of flattery. Of course, deer were still subject to the chase, and venison was a far more commonly eaten meat that it is now. However, anyone who has seen a herd of deer moving quietly through the dappled shadows of a Brown or a Repton park (if at Holkham, both) can hardly deny their superior elegance. Curiously, the horse, then a largely utilitarian animal, seems not to have been grazed near the house, whereas today it has almost as much status as the deer. If the animal did not have much visual status, much architectural effort was spent on the stables. Only a few deer houses were ever built, none by a major architect, and all had an additional use as an eye-catcher. No one now has the nerve (or preciosity) of Horace Walpole who grazed animals for the reasons described on page 51.

Estates which possessed natural lakes were regarded as especially fortunate. One with no water at all put its owner in a difficult position. Near or distant water appeared in all the best landscape paintings, but small and stagnant attempts by an owner to rectify the omission in his own domain were the object of ridicule. Laughter arose, too, where the position of a lake, or serpentine canal, too obviously played false the lie of the land. However, where the owner had a stream that could be dammed with taste and intelligence, the required lake could be treated. Indeed, all the most beautiful garden lakes (such as those at Blenheim, Stourhead, Luton Hoo

Lawn maintenance at Strawberry Hill, *c.* 1774.

An ingenious device from the *Encyclopaedia of Gardening*. In fact, the horse would have worn padded overshoes, and the hose-pipe would have been of leather.

The lake at West Wycombe: one of its several boats can be seen. Many lakes boasted a flotilla of pleasurecraft.

The lawn at West Wycombe: lawns played an important part in the way that gardens were used.

and Holkham) are artificial. Where a single dam has been enough, it is often disguised by heavy planting, by an island or by a twist in the design that puts it out of sight of all but the most inquisitive tourist. The far side of the dam often had a weir turned into a picturesque cascade, or the overflow escaped in the glittering and artificial darkness of a grotto. The dams all seem to have been well built. There is only one unverified report of a dam bursting, and that deliberately encouraged by an unscrupulous squire anxious to wash away a village offensively visible from his drawing-room. Where a single dam would have been too big or would have flooded too wide an area, several dams were made in sequence along a valley to produce a long narrow lake. Examples can be seen at Sheffield Park and Castle Howard, where the lakes date from 1795. Architectural features, especially bridges, were used to conceal some of the dams. Few visitors crossing it would realize that the water on one side might be several feet lower than that on the other.

In whatever way the water was held in place, there was absolutely nothing hit-or-miss in the way the lake was designed. All sites were very carefully surveyed before the dams were built. Ground was excavated or built up to produce a suitable shoreline, and, as a final check, white linen sheeting was often pinned along the entire proposed water-line to see how it looked. Marshall even suggested covering the whole area with linen, although the cost of such an exercise (even in windless weather) would have been enormous.

Plantings of lakeside banks, such a controversy in the late part of the period, has already been discussed. For planting the water itself, a wide range of species was known. During the early and middle part of the period, none was allowed into the lake, being kept to 'aquariums' in the flower garden. Even in the late part very little planting seems to have been done. The brilliancy of open water, having been obtained at such expense, was jealously guarded from both reed and lily. Waterfowl, both exotic and native, were encouraged for decoration and food, and fishing was a very important recreation (some charming fishing pavilions were built, for example at Studley Royal and Wardour Castle). For inland houses, the lake often provided the only source of fish for the table. No doubt many fishermen fished from perfectly orthodox boats, but beautifully lacquered Chinese junks or miniature galleons were a common sight on British lakes. Lord Byron's father had enough boats to conduct mock sea battles, and some lovely boats can be seen in paintings of the park and lakes at West Wycombe. The most outrageous boat of all, although used on a river not a lake, must have been the giant swan that the King used to commute between Kew and London. No means of locomotion is shown in Woollett's illustration (it can't, surely, have had artificial feet), and it must have been a murderous thing to steer in a high wind.

For those who chose not to risk themselves in decorative boats, even small gardens had any number of safe and winding pathways. That small gardens were often overburdened with them was a common complaint of all the design theorists. Many examples will be shown in the chapter on urban gardens. Loudon has a splendid suggestion for paths in a writer's garden, which he assumed would be small as few writers (even then) made much money. The path was a simple eclipse, so that the writer would be able to walk on and on, lost in thought or dreams of fame. Large gardens might have many miles of walks linking the various seats and pavilions. The paths were invariably gravelled (although sand, clinker and even crushed sea-shells had been tried), and where expense was no object, gravel from the pits at Kensington was brought in. Great care was taken to ensure good drainage, so that the paths could be used immediately after rain, and the flimsy shoes of the ladies not damaged. In contrast to today's paths, which are like walking on a shingle beach, the gravel was always bound with a fifth part of earth and then rolled. This gave a nice firm surface which drained rapidly but offered a foothold for weeds. The main weeding was done in the early spring after frost had loosened the surface.

Carriage roads were usually gravelled as well, but Repton and Nicol suggested that they be part metalled but with earth laid on top and then grassed. Posts were set at intervals to guide the coachman. The idea was to stop roads from detracting from the naturalness of the scene, and must have been quite common. They were certainly common enough to provoke ridicule. It was pointed out that, where this was done and the house left in a sea of grass, it looked as if no mortal had ever crossed the threshold. Whatever the surface, the narrow wheels of the carriages and the horses' hooves soon made the way very muddy. Where it was necessary for the garden walks to cross the carriage road, there were occasionally bridges or tunnels, so that the ladies could walk a circuit without any danger of mud.

In some ways, one of the most crucial elements, and the one which very clearly expresses the relationship between the garden and the outside world, is the boundary. Many writers, including Walpole, have seen in the first use of the ha-ha the beginning of the new landscape style. The walls of the old style, concealing and protective, vanished. The ha-ha, still protective and yet invisible to those on the inside, allowed an unfettered view outwards. A number of early examples have a mock-military air, complete with bastions and outworks, playful perhaps but partly symbolic of the times. Anyone who has lived in a Georgian house will be familiar with the remarkable security arrangements. In town houses with a front garden, even the outer gate could be kept closed from inside the house. Although ha-has could stop marauding cattle, few boundaries could stop marauding humans. The kitchen garden, with such rewarding spoils for the hungry, and much of the park, were liberally scattered with the man-traps already mentioned. There were two types: the normal one crushed very badly any limb it closed upon, but a slightly more 'humane' type was available, at extra cost, to finicky owners – these merely gave the shinbone a clean break.

Suburban gardens of mid-century were usually bounded with wooden palings. In various states of hybridity between gothic and Chinese, and painted white, their crispness was often derided. In spite of this, and in the usual way, the future lay with them. Railings, of whatever sort, were cheaper than ha-has. One man digging for a whole day could shift about nine cubic yards of reasonably workable soil. As the average-sized ha-ha had a vertical wall of six feet, that was about one and a half yards in distance. As the spoil had to be shifted elsewhere, carters had to be employed. The standard complement was one man for every twenty yards that the soil had to be carried. Furthermore, ha-has needed a stone or brick retaining wall on the vertical face, and so a number of masons were needed as well. Few ha-has were built after the 1770s. A slightly cheaper alternative was the sunk fence, for there was no vertical wall and so no building work. Either the bottom of the V-shaped ditch had a paling along its length, whose top remained below the general level of the land, or the slope nearest the house was planted with thorns spiny enough to deter entry. The plants were trimmed so that they did not grow into the view. The sunk fence was common to the end of the period, but where even this expense was too much, palings were used without a ditch and simply painted dark green or stone coloured. Deer parks needed quite high palings, and these were generally arranged to run through the belts and clumps of the landscape to stop them being too visible.

By the end of the period, with the increasing 'suburbanization' of taste, railings were no longer scoffed at but became integral parts of the garden-landscape. Numberless patterns were published, and while many were still in wood, the advances in cast-iron technology assured an astonishing prolixity of design. Many were remarkably elegant. By 1820 fencing had become a mania, dividing off each part of the garden and even becoming miniaturized as a fancy edging for paths, lawns and flowerbeds. This fussiness was adored throughout the nineteenth century, and gross plastic replicas of some of the patterns are still available. The fussiness could not conceal the symbolism of the re-emergent boundary, now created by a distant and technological industry and doing nothing to help local labour. I should like to end with a quotation from William Mason's *English Garden* of 1783, although the most vile boundary of all has been partly described in Chapter 14.

> Nor is that Cot of which fond Fancy draws
> This casual picture, alien from our theme.
> Revisit it at morn; its opening latch
> Tho' Penury and Toil within reside,
> Shall pour thee forth a youthful progeny
> Glowing with health and beauty: (such the dower
> Of equal heav'n) see, how the ruddy tribe

Throng round the threshold, and, with vacant gaze
Salute thee; call the loiterer into use,
And form of these they fence, the living fence
That graces what it guards . . .
                                    . . . Want, alas!
Has o'er their little limbs her livery hung
In many a tattered fold, yet still those limbs
Are shapely; their rude locks start from their brow,
Yet, on that open brow, its dearest throne,
Sits sweet Simplicity. Ah, clothe the troop
In such russet garb as best befits
Their pastoral office; let the leathern scrip
Swing at their side, tip their crooks with steel,
And braid their hat with rushes, then to each
Assign his station. . . .

In France, similar fantasies were soon to be wrecked.

The gardens

21. Urban gardens

Cities have always had gardens. In Britain, before the eighteenth century, their integration into it was usually haphazard. Those of the private citizen were often narrow strips behind house or shop. The main open spaces that remained had almost always once been royal hunting parks. By the seventeenth century these had all become dedicated to the recreation and exercise of the populace. From the mid-1600s the great urban developments of the capital (and they were great in extent, usually great in profit and almost always visually marvellous) had gardens which were planned and indeed thoroughly integrated into the design not only of the squares and crescents that surrounded them but of the internal layout of the houses themselves.

The great squares of London, Edinburgh and Dublin, as well as those of the elegant spa towns, were all descendants of a square built in Paris in the late sixteenth century. The Place des Vosges (then called the Place Royale) was the first piece of urban planning that reduced the chaos of individual caprice to a single cohesive form. Four rows of houses were built facing a large square of ground, each house subordinate in design to that of the entire square. The appearance is very restrained, immensely elegant, was sometimes equalled but never, I think, surpassed. The central garden, now with regularly planted trees, very dusty gravel walks, drinking-fountains and the inevitable late-nineteenth-century statue, was originally planned for tournaments and jousts and all the excitements of feudal state. The squares of London and Edinburgh were not planned for anything so exotic. In London, the first comparable venture was the piazza at Covent Garden. This was designed by Inigo Jones and was built in the 1630s. It followed the lead of the Place Royale fairly closely, although it was smaller and less complete. One side was taken up with the Earl of Bedford's garden, and another was given over to the church that can still be seen. None of the houses survives, and the arcaded buildings that can be seen are modern. A painting of the central green space done in about 1649 shows that it was just

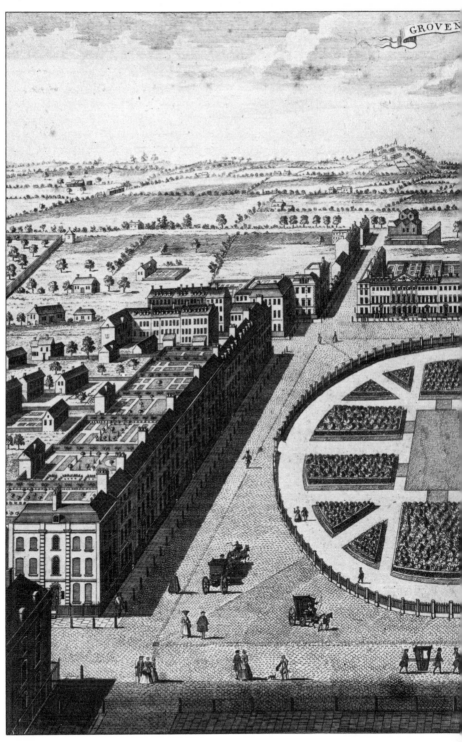

Many town gardens were remarkably conservative: Grosvenor Square (London) in 1735, with equally formal private gardens visible behind the houses.

grass and straight gravel walks, with only a simple wooden rail.

Such a splendid way of combining high population densities with considerable elegance was soon taken up. Other squares were built. Contemporary prints well into the next century show the gardens to have been similar in layout (and presumably in use) to that of the piazza. Sutton Nicholl's engraving of Grosvenor Square shows a nice circular garden, but with more elaborate and more secure railings. It must soon have occurred to both the occupants of the houses and the developers of the estate that the gardens would make a splendid private amenity, if railings and gates were put up to keep out less fortunate mortals and their horses. The enclosed space could then become a garden in the fullest sense of the word, and then become subject to the same changes in taste.

Thus the Georgian city came to contain three main types of garden: the private garden behind each individual house and available only to the house's inhabitants, the semi-public gardens in the squares available only to those whose houses overlooked it, and the fully public gardens which were mostly survivals from an earlier age. A fourth type, and one which played a much greater part in the literature of the age than the other three, was the public pleasure garden that charged for admission. London had Vauxhall, Ranelagh and several others; Bath had Sydney and Spring Gardens. Although they played rather little part in the development of garden design, they will be mentioned briefly later. Botanic gardens and nursery gardens will not be dealt with.

The private and semi-public gardens related to the disposition of rooms in town houses. The usual terrace-house design of three bays (allowing a ground floor of two windows and a doorway) had all the public rooms at the front. The front ground-floor room was generally the dining-room, the first-floor level being devoted to a drawing-room, or drawing-room and dressing-room. This enabled the wealth, taste and individuality of the owners to be displayed to the world from windows in a façade where individuality had been suppressed in favour of the grand design. From inside, the owner could look out into a wide expanse of highly kept garden. Private rooms at the back of the house, away from the noise of the street criers and of hooves and steel-rimmed wheels on cobblestones, looked out over the diversity of the small private gardens. It was an ideal arrangement. The only suggestion that the desire for show was more important than the desire for quiet privacy was that, in circumstances where both back and front of the house were equally quiet, public rooms remained at the front even when the best view was at the back. Perhaps it was simply that public rooms were felt to be better placed overlooking public places, and vice versa.

There are very few of the private gardens still intact. Being small, they are easily revamped; being urban, they are subject to all sorts of urban pressure; and being privately owned, they are easily destroyed. Many vanished when

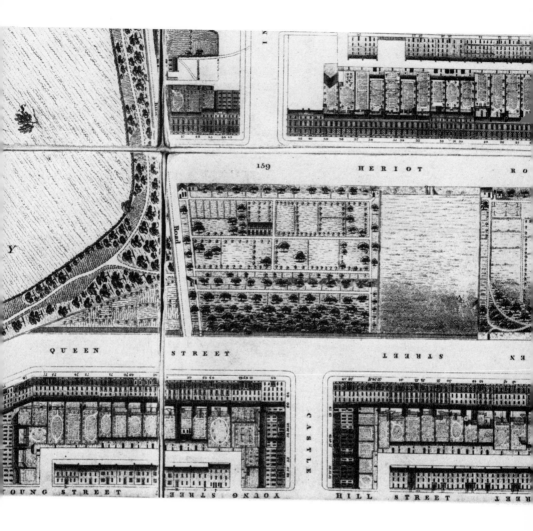

Above: Kirkwood's street plan of Edinburgh's New Town (1819) shows private gardens and the as yet un-landscaped semi-public ones.

Left: A typical semi-public garden design with a central pavilion (e), flower beds, lawns and a surrounding shrubbery.

Victorian owners found their houses too small. Landlords or feudal superiors would often not allow any upward building, and, of course, no expansion could take place sideways. The private garden was the only suitable space. Mews, if the terrace were sufficiently grand to have them, were often taken over by small businesses if the area declined at all in its fortunes. The factories then invaded the garden. The effects of this can be seen in all city centres. A more modern menace is tarmac, for where houses have become offices, employees need somewhere to park their cars. Consequently, most evidence of their appearance and use is indirect, either from contemporary maps and prints or from surveys and occasionally architects' plans.

The function of these private gardens is not immediately clear. They seem to have been only rarely productive of fruit and vegetables. Most big cities were amply supplied with these by the extensive market gardens that surrounded them. Certainly, few original fruit trees are ever found in them today, and indeed there are often few large trees of any species. None of these gardens ever seems to be mentioned in any memoir or novel. Furthermore, usual access to them was from the servants' quarters in the basement. Visitors would not have been shown through such ungenteel regions, often unfamiliar to the owners themselves. Although it is nowadays common to see steps from one of the back ground-floor rooms, these are invariably a recent addition to the house. In Scotland, these private gardens were often called 'drying greens', a term still occasionally in use. In many of them can still be seen the elegant urn-topped iron poles from which the washing-lines were strung. So we can see them in use by the laundress, who 'jobbed' in the same way as most urban gardeners, hanging out sheets, napery and dismantled articles of clothing.

Nevertheless contemporary maps, of both London and Edinburgh, show that the gardens had quite a diversity of layout and were by no means just grass and clothes-poles. Only the largest ones attempted anything in the landscape way, the surrounding urban environment precluding much Arcadian fantasy. While as late as the 1750s their appearance was very four-square and formal, after that date their layouts became less dependent on geometric beds and topiary. As the plots were generally long and narrow, a gravel path described an oval, an oblong or a figure-of-eight, that took up most of the length of the garden. The central part enclosed by the path was generally lawn, and the outer corners flowerbeds or shrubbery. Most of them are similar to an arrangement suggested by Loudon: "If he [an author] can afford any other garden that a pot of mint, [he] should surround his plot with an oval path, that he may walk on without end and without any sensible change in the position of his body." Less reflective owners may have preferred rectangular paths. The gardens were at least used for personal and private exercise.

Of the planting of them, equally little seems yet to be known. We do know that evergreens were always popular, especially because they could survive the polluted atmosphere. Hollies, laurels, myrtles, yews and arbor-vitae were common. Box remained a popular edging for paths throughout the period and was bought in considerable yardages. However, as every city supported a large number of nurserymen, all with bulging catalogues, the over-all range of species must have been much wider. The nurseries cannot have been maintained solely by the local magnates planting up their country gardens in the latest taste. One clue can be found on the walls dividing garden from garden, where one can still often find the iron pegs that would have once held up honeysuckle, jasmine and the rest.

Of course, some indisputably urban gardens were beyond normal restrictions of design and planting. Carlton House gardens, first laid out by Kent for Lord Carlton, altered by Brown and then improved by Holland for the Prince Regent, were almost large enough to pretend to Arcadia. They were full of winding walks and wavy-edged flowerbeds and with a peripheral belt of trees and shrubs. This latter was not a success, being too thinly planted and so offering little privacy. Repton suggested several alterations, including opening up a number of views of the city without allowing the curious to see in. Buckingham House, too, had a large garden. First laid out in the 1750s by Robinson, it was still being altered in the early nineteenth century, when 'House' was soon to become 'Palace'. *The Gardeners' Magazine* reviewed the changes unkindly in one of the series of articles on suburban gardens. The writer was particularly horrified at the adulation in the rest of the Press of the newly formed hillocks (one journalist apparently comparing them with "the noble peaks of the Pennines"). He also thought the situation of the house "dreadful" and felt, with little real sympathy, that the lake then forming would rapidly carry off the House of Hanover. Malaria from its fetid vapours was to be the cause. The author, almost certainly Loudon himself to judge from the scale of the suggestion, went on to provide an alternative: a vast palace to be built on even vaster terraces on the banks of the Thames. The view would be superb, the terraces were to be planted like the hanging gardens of Babylon, and the location would be healthy. He plainly had no idea that the river would become more of a hazard to health than a mere garden pond.

For those who could not afford such spaces but could afford a fine house, the semi-public gardens offered at least an approach to similar splendours. Only a few squares now look at all as they once did. Many, especially in London, have now become fully public spaces and are usually over-used, underplanted and thoroughly municipal. A few of the finest, though, retain much of their original layout, much of their original function and a good deal of their social exclusivity. These semi-public gardens, apart from providing a nice green view from the drawing-room and dining-room, were used for gentle exercise (those needing something more energetic could ride horses along Rotten Row in London, the Meadows in Edinburgh and the Sidney Gardens in Bath), for equally gentle repose on one of the many graceful iron seats provided, or as a safe (and distant) place for the children to play. Naturally, the regulations that governed the running of each garden ensured that only social equals ever met and that there was no chance of being offended by the presence of an inferior.

Such laws were usually made by a committee of householders whose property adjoined the garden. The garden itself was usually the property of the leaseholder or feudal superior (in Scotland), although there are a few examples where the freehold is owned jointly by all householders allowed to use it. In all cases, admission to the garden was by key, and an annual charge on each one was made to cover the cost of upkeep and improvement. All but the most unsociable or penurious householders took keys, but where the income from these was still inadequate, residents in neighbouring streets were allowed the privilege of paying. Of course, only those streets with sufficient social *ton* were considered. In Edinburgh, Drummond Place gardens (one of those owned by its keyholders) are open only to some inhabitants of the square, and only those with first-floor apartments on adjacent streets. Such flats were, and still are, more expensive than those on other floors and are more grandly proportioned and expensively detailed. However, it is more common nowadays in other gardens for any applicant who can pay the fee to be allowed entry.

Few of the minutes from the various committees have survived. One set that has, relates to Princes Street gardens, again in Edinburgh. These gardens were, until the 1830s, extremely fashionable indeed. They were so much used that the gate locks were worn out six years after the gardens had opened. The gardens were first formed in 1818 and opened two years later, after various difficulties with one of the contractors (of the many thousands of his trees planted, only one hundred of them survived, although he weathered the scandal well enough to become Lord Provost). The keys were advertised at four pounds a year. At first only lawyers applied, but in a few years the gardens became very fashionable as titled people moved from the old town to the new. There were soon complaints that keyholders were lending keys to the most distant of their connections, and this was soon followed by the discovery of a thriving business in counterfeit keys. Even common soldiers found their way in. Eventually, gatemen had to be employed at eighteen shillings a week, and a policeman on Sundays at two shillings. By 1828 various houses in Princes Street were unoccupied as people moved to the newer and grander parts of the developing city. Soon the houses were subdivided, and haberdashers and confectioners moved in. There they remain, and Princes Street gardens are open to the world. Of other Edinburgh gardens, only those of the superb Moray Place retain their original layout, though they no longer boast the hot-bed that once must have produced many exotic seedlings. Incidentally, there was often quite a gap between the finishing of the houses and the enclosing and development of the central gardens, the illustration on page 179 showing part of them still used as drying greens and market gardens.

In London, while new squares were completed from the mid-seventeenth century onwards (Grosvenor Square in 1695, Portman Square in 1766 and Manchester Square ten years later), the largest number of squares date from after 1800. Although the name of William Kent has been (incorrectly) associated with Grosvenor Square, no early garden layouts seem to have been designed by well-known practitioners. The first to involve himself with urban schemes was Humphry Repton, who did Russell, Cadogan and Bloomsbury Squares (the latter with its original plan intact). Russell Square, planted in 1810, was widely criticized for being overplanted, although Repton had intended the planting to be thinned as it matured. Perhaps this criticism stopped his plans for Sloane Square coming to fruition. This had been planted up with regular beds so that it could act as a botanic garden for the edification of the local inhabitants. Because of its long and narrow site, he suggested a long winding pool, with equally winding walks and natural-looking plantations. One naturalistic scheme that was carried out was in Edwardes Square in Kensington. This was also one of the rare instances where a painter was called in as designer, in this case a now-forgotten gentleman named Aiglio.

Very few semi-public gardens made any attempt at naturalism. The most common plan was merely an enlarged copy of the private house-gardens. Many, in London and Edinburgh, were unashamedly formal and symmetrical, but always with outer belts of trees and shrubs to provide some privacy. The inner lawn usually had typical late-Georgian flowerbeds. Loudon, with his neo-classical passion for ancient splendours (usually Babylonian, perhaps under the influence of John Martin), suggested that town gardens should be terraced like Isola Bella (or Babylon), with vaults beneath being used as warehouses or cattle markets. I am not sure how the chaste squares of Bloomsbury or Belgravia would have looked with such moo-ing ziggurats in their middles.

Before Repton introduced the whole range of exotic species into urban gardens, most seem to have been rather dingily planted. He engineered the switch from evergreen to deciduous species, for he felt that the latter had the advantage of casting their sooty leaves once a year. However short a time their new ones remained shiny, evergreens kept their grimy ones for several years. The only objection raised was that as the best town houses were used only during the winter, the town gardens should be 'winter gardens'. Perhaps in the early nineteenth century 'the season' had become extended. Certainly, there was a considerable emphasis on the flowerbeds, and fashionable gardens demanded fashionable species. The beds would have been quite as heavily loaded with colour (except for the widely planted beds of yellowish-green mignonette) as they are today.

The urban population who had no access to the type of gardens described above did have alternatives. These were naturally most diverse in London. The royal parks offered the largest and most decorative spaces, were widely used and were free. No other city boasted comparable facilities: the royal park of Holyrood showed Nature quite unadorned and seems to have played no part in the formal social life of the city. The great parks of London and its environs (St James's, Hyde, Green, Kensington, Richmond and later Regent's Parks) have always attracted the leading designers of the day, although none of them seems to have been the site of any major innovation. Even if Kent went to the much-derided lengths of planting dead trees in Hyde Park, the Serpentine was only bent, rather than serpentine, and was not especially advanced for the year of its completion (1730). The canal in St James's Park was very conservative, not being serpentinized until 1827. The formal 'round' pond in Kensington Gardens still survives. Even the ridiculed 'Merlin's Cave' with its waxen Merlin lasted well into less artificial days. In provincial and less elevated circles such grotesque waxworks remained in fashion, a similarly equipped hermitage being one of the sideshows in Bath's Sydney Gardens in 1825. There was also a 'Merlin's Cave' there but this time without Merlin. Although more a place of promenade than a garden in the strict sense, the Mall at St James's was used by both Court and populace. The hours were between midday and two o'clock, and again after dinner (eaten in the later afternoon for much of the period), but then in full dress. The Mall lost fashion in the 1780s because the Queen preferred Green Park, in spite of its lack of water. Hyde Park was the only place for a horse or a carriage until Regent's Park came into use in 1810.

Farmland until 1784, a number of architect-planners devised schemes for Regent's Park. Most of them simply divided it into plots for villas, with little left for public amenity. Nash's splendid plan was finally adopted, and building began in the early nineteenth century. However splendid the results (rendered less so by the absence of the proposed palace to terminate the ceremonial way from the city), Loudon still considered the area too much restricted by the number of private villas. His own wildly grandiose suggestion for a new amenity was for an immense carriage-road to encircle London completely. It crossed the Thames on iron pillars high enough to let all shipping pass beneath. The visitor could have encompassed everything in the city in a day; the age of the tourist would really have arrived. However keen Loudon may have been on unimpeded spaces in London parks, his suggestions for the Holyrood Park in Edinburgh were in direct contradiction. He proposed a spiral road ascending Arthur's Seat to the top, and a similar one descending. Each lozenge of ground enclosed by the intersecting avenues would form the site of the same sort of villas he so disliked in London. No doubt, had the scheme happened, there would have been some marvellously rocky late-Georgian gardens, but the traffic problems would have been horrendous.

London, too, contained almost all of the commercial pleasure grounds. These, in spite of the immense sums of money spent on planting and landscaping, played very little part in the history of gardening, although they must have represented for many people their only contact with gardening 'taste'. The two most famous ones in London have already been mentioned, but there was also a large selection of wells and spas, all with fashionable gardens. All of them seem to have been an amalgam of Arcadia and fairground. Balls, supper-parties, concerts and routs were held in them, and, for those determined on a full day's pleasure, there were even musical breakfasts. Each garden vied with the others in the splendour of its entertainments, its fireworks and its exhibitions. Among the latter, Ranelagh staged an amazing 'Eruption of Mount Etna' that required a wooden replica of the volcano eighty feet high. (An equally amazing exhibition was made by the Chevalier d'Eon, who fenced there publicly. In private, he exhibited himself to those anxious to discover his true gender, upon which no final decision ever seems to have been taken. He was even examined by a covey of aristocratic ladies who were determined to find out.) Pleasure gardens of this sort had an ancient history. Some must have been very splendid. A number of marbles in Lord Burlington's collection at Chiswick had been dug up from the refuse of one that had been closed down. It had become too notorious for the authorities to tolerate. All the gardens had many visitors who hoped to make more money there than they had paid to get in. The other important garden, Vauxhall, even gave rise to a noun.

Bath's similar garden had, as its full name, 'Sydney Gardens Vauxhall'. These, with the full paraphernalia of 'Ancient Dilapidated Castle', 'Cosmorama' (which cost sixpence to see), grottoes and aviaries, also had a carriage ride on its perimeter. A six-month subscription for a saddle-horse was twelve shillings, and that for a grand four-horse carriage (which was absurd, for the garden was by no means large) was one pound and ten shillings. To get in in the first place cost twelve shillings per person for six months; a single entry cost sixpence. One certainly got value for money: the maze was twice as big as the one at Hampton Court, and all the other bits and pieces were so closely jumbled that a visitor can scarcely have left one before being enveloped in the next. However absurd this may have seemed, with night to obscure the narrow confines, it must have looked splendid during a 'gala'. John Kew, in a puff he wrote for the gardens in 1825, said: "The gardens are beautifully illuminated by upwards of fifteen thousand variegated lamps. . . ." Enthusiasm might have been damped by learning that they were "tastefully disposed in appropriate figures, mottoes and figurative embellishments". Sydney Gardens still exist, marred by a railway line and time. The hotel, a rather modest one, that owned them still faces down Great Pulteney Street but is now a museum.

22. Suburban gardens

"But the triumph of his genius [the overweening villa-owner] was seen in the disposition of his gardens, which contained everything in less than two acres of ground. At your first entrance, the eye is saluted with a yellow serpentine river, stagnating through a beautiful valley which extends near twenty yards in length. . . ." Thus runs part of an article in a magazine of 1753. Many writers poked similarly mocking fingers throughout the rest of the period. Yet city suburbs were then, and often still are, undoubtedly pleasant places to live. For some reason, the word 'suburban' is now often used as a term of abuse, with strong social overtones. 'Suburban', in the sense used in this chapter, is a term of function rather than of social class and covers a wide range of wealth and social position. People who lived in Georgian suburbs were tied to a city because of their income, their function or their inclination. However, the first of these enabled them to live amid most of the amenities of the countryside. None, or only a tiny part, of their income was derived from the country, and no suburban house is the centre of an estate. Suburbs are also dependent on transport. In the eighteenth century it required some degree of wealth to have the necessary carriages and horses. It required wealth, too, to buy sufficient land to provide a pastoral illusion. By the end of the period, with a much wider distribution of wealth, many more people could afford both.

Suburban gardens, because divorced from the needs of profit, because small (although we shall see that ideas of scale have changed somewhat) and because often owned by people very much concerned with being 'in the fashion', have played an important part in the history of garden design. Three technically suburban gardens have already been described in some detail: Chiswick, Strawberry Hill and Pope's garden at Twickenham. All three owners were rich (Lord Burlington extremely so), and all three moved in aristocratic society (although Pope's father had been a draper). By the third quarter of the period, the idea of suburban living was both possible and popular.

Villas, if rather smaller than the three mentioned, became the suburban house *par excellence*. They were a staple article of design for almost every architect. The first book of villa designs was published in 1768 by John Crunden, and many followed in subsequent years. Villas soon became very middle class indeed. However, in the 1770s the only possible landscape style was that of the current aristocratic mode. Exemplified by, say, Holkham, this was suitable only for the widest spaces. The villa-owner, not unnaturally, was anxious to copy it but, instead of taking one or two of the most suitable elements, tried to cram everything into the available space. It did not work. *Columella* (by Richard Graves) mocks the *nouveau riche* Mr Nonsuch for packing "a large shrubbery, a small serpentine river over which was thrown a Chinese bridge of considerable diameter . . . a Chinese pagoda, a gothic temple, a grotto, a root house, a hermitage, a Chinese tub or two by the waterside" all into one acre (obviously he was not *that* rich), as well as a summerhouse in one corner and a barn with a gothic spire in the other.

The problem was not solved until the last phase of Georgian gardening began, and the solution seems to have been inherently suburban. Of course a number of other factors were important: the nostalgia for formalism, aristocratic ideas of 'the Picturesque' and the immense increase in horticultural material. Curiously, there is no 'type locality' for the new style. It is impossible to point to a few particular gardens, as one can with the earlier landscape styles, and say that they are the first examples. This is perhaps the result of the immense increase in the publication of books and magazines. Because debate was so widespread and so informed, the new style seems gradually to have come into existence in literally hundreds of gardens, and by the time certain ones became famous as exemplars, no one knew which had been the first. Although Repton designed many quite small gardens, I don't think that his name can be associated with the formation of the new style. His talent was for the elegant application of already accepted ideas. Certainly, by the time the *Encyclopaedia* was published, Loudon was able to illustrate many interesting and highly developed layouts.

The first book devoted to the suburban garden was Walter Nicol's *Villa Garden Directory* of 1809. This was very successful and was in a fourth edition by 1823. Even he finds it necessary to point out that, "To pretend to represent in a few acres the buildings, plantations and waters of a *Place* is absurd. Yet we sometimes meet with the belt, the shrubbery, the double approach, the lawn, the kitchen garden, the court of offices, the prospect towers and even the lake, huddled together in a very, very extra-ordinary manner." He thought an equally silly error was "that of bounding the whole with a connected belt of shrubbery, or other plantation, leaving the house in a small open paddock, unadorned by a plant of any kind". He suggested that it was better to have clumps, groups and single specimens along the perimeter, with the actual boundary being kept by a green-painted railing or

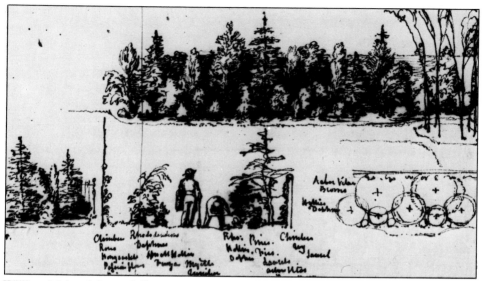

William Mulready's carefully worked-out design for his London garden.

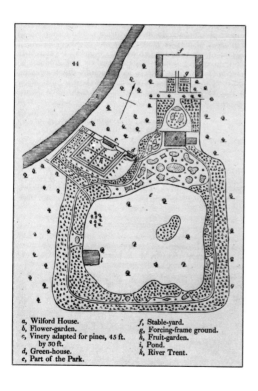

a, Wilford House.
b, Flower-garden.
c, Vinery adapted for pines, 45 ft.
   by 30 ft.
d, Green-house.
e, Part of the Park.
f, Stable-yard.
g, Forcing-frame ground.
h, Fruit-garden.
i, Pond.
k, River Trent.

Left: Wilford Hall's Victorian-looking flower beds are concentrated near the house but can be found scattered throughout the landscape.

Below: Design for a suburban front garden of the 1820s, with beds for annual flowers set in grass and gravel.

wire fence. Even where there was not a clutter of bits and pieces, he felt that "The surface [of the lawn] should not be cut up by a multitude of gravel walks, screwed and twisted in all directions, as we all too frequently notice. A walk skirting the boundary . . . will be found sufficient."

Design was partly dependent on the scale of the garden. Loudon (as well as Marshall) adopted an elaborate grading of suburban gardens which is of interest. The "smaller suburban garden" was thought to be an eighth to half an acre in size, with a front garden of grass and flowerbeds of annuals. The back one was just lawn with a gravel walk, and a few vegetables hidden away. The main planting would be of evergreens. Only a jobbing gardener would be employed. Slightly higher on the social ladder were "tradesmen's villas". These, with grounds from a quarter to a full acre, boasted elaborate flowerbeds in front. With no kitchen garden to maintain, the gardener was usually a hybrid sort of servant, also acting as groom or footman. For those owners of similar means but without the disadvantage of having to earn it in trade, were the full "suburban, or citizen's villas". Loudon characterizes the owners as "if not more wealthy than tradesmen, possessing more of the taste and *ton* of good society." One man who probably fits into this category was the painter William Mulready. The sketches he made for the proposed plantings of his London home survive and are of the greatest interest, listing as they do the species to be included. They are very advanced. A Scottish example is the garden attached to the house where this book has been written. The house was built for Daniel Ellis, who published some early papers on plant physiology and was instrumental in setting up the Experimental Gardens (now part of the Royal Botanic Garden) of the Caledonian Horticultural Society. He was an enthusiastic collector of new fruit varieties, and a number of the trees he planted are still remarkably productive. The original layout still survives. However, neither of these examples fulfils Loudon's expectation of size, both being too small. He felt that for people to have *ton*, their garden should be from one to ten acres in size, and that a master gardener should be employed to keep all of it in the highest point of elegance. Only the most select flowers and trees would be grown, colours and odours selected to please the ladies of the house or any other particularly fastidious person. However, it was also felt that great care should be taken not to be as grand as the garden of a real villa, let alone a 'place'. The lists given by Nicol of suitably 'subordinate' plants are not all that dull. They include purple beech, the weeping birch, lucombe oak, tulip trees and walnuts.

It was the larger late-Georgian villas, however, that received most attention in literature. Many were designed by reputable architects, and their owners were often wealthy enough to engage the services of a landscape designer. A suburban villa on this scale might be set in anything from ten to a hundred acres and was expected to have a head gardener and staff, hothouses, vineries and the rest. To judge from the complaints of many garden writers, the owners (often "opulent commercial men") did not generally engage the skilled professionals. It must have been far too much fun designing a garden on that scale to let the pleasure slip away to someone else. In any case, the general movement of the age was to individualism in taste. The only risk in taking the responsibility oneself was to be visited by Loudon looking for material for one of his "Calls at Suburban Gardens" articles. As we have already seen, he included gardens of such social elevation as Buckingham House, and as far afield as Windsor, but he could be equally rude about far more modest establishments.

At an intermediate level, Dropmore, where the new style had been taken up by Lady Grenville, boasted the biggest and finest parterres that Loudon had seen. He also said that she was "so enthusiastically fond of gardening pursuits, [that she] cannot avoid pushing the taste further . . .". The result was that various beds of geraniums, salvias, heliotropes and fuchsias were scattered throughout the grounds without rhyme or reason. Lady Grenville also had a curious habit (considering her wealth) of turning every piece of junk she found about the house or estate into fanciful urns and pedestals. All these were gaily planted. Loudon was not amused. However, no matter what the failings of the lady's particular taste, the garden does show a more general weakness: the return to favour of small formal elements (which is what these rather scrappy parterres were) lacked any powerful and organizing over-all structure. The plan of Wilford Hall in Nottinghamshire shows a comparable and entirely typical example. In this, one can see the flowerbeds beginning to seep away from the house into more distant parts of the garden. The flowerbeds in Maria Jackson's book, whether 'Etruscan' or informal, show a similar weakness of design. The masculine vigour that had energized formalism in the seventeenth century had gone. Perhaps it had been sapped by too much sentiment, leaving formalism without form.

Between the suburban villas so far described and the houses that were the hubs of landed estates, came two rather interesting categories. The *ferme ornée* has already been discussed. Although it was still popular in the early nineteenth century, it had by then a strong rival. This too, for some reason, had a French name. The *cottage ornée* was almost a new species of building. Bred from the *ferme ornée* by some sort of cross with a garden pavilion, the word *cottage* could be quite misleading. Although the ground had no pretence whatever to productivity, the house was often quite large. In style it was usually 'Picturesque', with a low thatched roof supported on vaguely Doric rustic columns (all very primitivist). Occasionally they were in a rather simplified gothic. Papworth designed some amusing examples in both styles, some with quite grand interiors. John Soane also produced some, and, of course, Nash built other famous examples. The owners of this new breed were a new breed themselves. Papworth described the *cottage*

An elegant *cottage ornée* designed by J. B. Papworth.

ornée as the residence "of men of study, science or leisure". These disciplines were not themselves new, but the first two had become the hobbies of a new class of person, who was more or less fortunate to have only a genteel private income. Curiously, too, the houses seem rarely to have been designed for full family life. Bachelors, sets of spinsters, couples whose means and appetites were too slender to support children, seem to have been the inhabitants. (I know of two that were built as summer retreats for duchesses.) This sub-rural world, where what were only hobbies became the mainstay of life, naturally lavished attention on gardens. As we have seen, Papworth produced all sorts of non-botanical decoration. His illustrations show the gardens packed with brilliantly flowered plantings, none of which would look out of place on a modern seed packet. Some of Repton's designs of this period are entirely comparable.

Marshall's more serious taste offered an alternative, however difficult to achieve. For instance, nothing

> should appear vulgar, nor should simplicity be pared down to baldness; everything whimsical or expensive should be studiously avoided. Chasteness and frugality should appear in every part. . . . If a taste for botany leads to a collection of native shrubs and flowers, a shrubbery will be requisite but, in this, everything should be native. A gaudy exotic should not be admitted; nor should the lawn be kept close shaven; its flowers should be permitted to blow, and the herbage, when mown, ought to be carried off and applied to a useful purpose.

What that might be he does not say. Incidentally, Marshall adds another rather similar category, that of the 'hunting box'. This, a self-consciously masculine equivalent of the *cottage ornée*, was to be surrounded with absolutely hardy evergreens, such as box, holly and lauristinus, and good sensible trees such as oak and beech. Through these, suites of paddocks were to be seen from the windows (in which handsome mares should graze!).

Mansions and demesnes

23. *Mansions and demesnes*

However many urban and suburban gardens have been lost to us, the loss is perhaps softened by the numbers of Georgian country gardens that remain. Here, too, major losses have been sustained and are still occurring. Gardens are expensive things to maintain, and the number of owners who can afford such splendid luxuries continues to diminish. Considering how much society has changed between 1830 and the present day, perhaps we should be very surprised that so many are left, and of what quality. Although some owners find that they have to return their parks and pleasure grounds to agriculture, or to allow them to vanish beneath housing developments, an increasing number are opening them to the general public. This is in many ways a splendid development, and we must hope that the rewards for opening will be sufficient to compensate the owners for their loss of privacy and to stop them otherwise destroying a unique part of British culture.

The pleasures of garden visiting have long been known. While, in the early part of the period, the visitors were usually other country house owners, by the 1760s, visiting had become a much more socially widespread diversion. Some of the most famous gardens had to have specially built inns to accommodate the curious. By the end of the period very large numbers of gardens were freely open. For instance, of the forty-six major Yorkshire gardens, eleven were open, and these included Bramham, Studley Royal and Harewood. In Surrey, of the forty-six gardens included in Loudon's list, nine were open (Deepdene, Painshill and Claremont among them). In Middlesex, Marble Hill (without much of a garden), Strawberry Hill, Gunnersbury, Chiswick, Holland House and Syon House were all available to view. There are very few houses anywhere that were then open but are now closed. Some, of course, have become more public, now being owned by the State, the National Trust or municipalities, or having become golf clubs and hotels.

Although a few houses described in the following pages are, if strictly considered, suburban, most would have easily passed Loudon's and

The house stands isolated from the stables (top left) and kitchen garden (bottom right).

Marshall's tests for mansions and demesnes. The smaller houses would have been owned by (to use Loudon's phrase) "independent gentlemen of middling fortune". There would have been a kitchen garden of more than an acre, with possibly a flower garden attached of a third the size. The wider pleasure ground might contain ten to twelve acres. However, the most important element, and the one that most alluded to the social status of the owner, was the lawn or park. The smallest possible size was twenty acres, and the largest that could be owned without one being accused of pretension was five times that size. Certainly, at that scale some attempt at landscape gardening could be made. Loudon comments that the standard of upkeep on such estates was very variable. Perhaps that was because they could be owned by families on the decline, as well as those that were rising. There seems to have been no such problem for the fortunate owners of the mansion residence. Every garden seems to have been well maintained. These grand houses were entitled to be called 'place', 'hall', 'court' or 'castle'. The staff would have included a secretary, a house steward (with his own free house and £150 to £300 a year), a land steward, a bailiff, a head gardener with several foremen and his own horse and chaise. As well as the kitchen and flower garden, he would have supervised a pleasure ground of twenty to a hundred acres, and a park with a minimum of five hundred. Naturally, there was no maximum size. Very few of the gardens listed in the following pages are still run on such a scale.

Little remains to be said. Most of the book has been about the way in which these gardens were made and used. The gazetteer that follows describes many splendid examples of Georgian gardens, with particular emphasis on those that can easily be visited. There are, of course, many other beautiful gardens that are not listed. It must be remembered that every Georgian house will have had a garden that was once loved by its owner. Not all of them have been famous, fewer still are much documented. An immense amount of research remains to be done, and many beauties remain to be rediscovered. I hope that the foregoing chapters will encourage the reader to explore the landscape and that they will offer at least some keys to the interpretation of the gardens within it.

A Gazetteer of Georgian Gardens

The houses marked with an asterisk have gardens which are frequently open to the public. The local Press will usually show details of opening times and public transport services. The nearest town is given as a means of locating the garden; in a few cases this may be in a county different from that given for the house.

*ALNWICK CASTLE
Alnwick, Northumberland
A superb Brown landscape of the 1760s, around a spectacularly sited house. The park, without too much later alteration, is studded with garden buildings by Robert and John Adam. Hulne Priory is especially good.

*ALTHORP
Northampton, Northamptonshire
A fine house. When Loudon described the gardens, it was still moated, with bridges leading into the formal gardens. These were replaced with a Brown-style landscape designed by Henry Holland

*ALTON TOWERS
near Uttoxeter, Staffordshire
A remarkable example of late-Georgian excess, now thankfully rather thinned out. Planned by the Earl of Shrewsbury from 1814, it has buildings by Papworth (in both Greek and gothic) and others. It also has the famous island pagoda, as well as the less well-known Druids' temple, cascades, fountains and much else. The house is now ruined.

AMPTON HALL
Bury, Suffolk
This and the neighbouring property of Livermere shared an artificial lake. It was Livermere that had a large painting in the Dutch style at the lake's end.

*ANTONY HOUSE
Plymouth, Devonshire
A magnificent park by Repton, in his grandest manner, from 1793 to 1803. The terracing around the house is probably of the same date.

*ARBURY HALL
Nuneaton, Warwickshire
A fine park with the lake almost up to the walls of the house. Sanderson Miller may have advised on the gardens when he was engaged in alterations to the house from 1750.

*ASHRIDGE PARK
Hemstead, Buckinghamshire
Always a famous garden. The park is by Brown, and the fourteen acres of flower garden by Repton, designed in 1814.

Alton Towers: one of the most remarkable greenhouses in any late-Georgian garden.

ASKE HALL
Richmond, North Yorkshire
Kent worked here, on the quite
splendid gothic folly. It was built
between 1725 and 1758. He may also
have advised on the rest of the park.

ASTON PARK
Oswestry, Shropshire
Much admired in the early
nineteenth century and said to be in
"the very best taste".

*ATTINGHAM PARK
Attingham, Shropshire
The park was designed by Repton in
1798. There is a nice gothic
eye-catcher.

*AUDLEY END
Saffron Walden, Essex
A finely wooded and watered park
done by Brown in the 1760s. Repton
advised on various alterations.
Interesting remains of the kitchen
garden.

*BADMINTON
Malmesbury, Avon
A quite splendid garden with a
complicated history. Kent worked
here from 1746 (and designed a
marvellous pavilion). Various
schemes were then undertaken by
Wright, including much planting and
more garden buildings. He was
followed by Brown, who left many of
the earlier avenues intact.
'Improvements' continued into the
nineteenth century. The park was
originally nine miles in
circumference.

BALBIRNIE HOUSE
Glenrothes, Fife
A good Scottish example of the
Brown style. It was carried out by his
imitator, White the Younger, from
1815. However, the basis was an
earlier landscape by Robinson of
thirty years before.

*BARGANY PARK
Girvan, Ayrshire
Much admired by Loudon.

BARWICK PARK
Yeovil, Somerset
A once-splendid mid-period park,
complete with some amusing follies
and a sinister grotto.

BAVIS MOUNT
Southampton, Hampshire
Once the site of a good proto-
landscape designed by the Earl of
Peterborough.

BEAUDESART
Stafford, Staffordshire
Now demolished, the house was a
splendid fake castle set in gardens
that had been 'done over' by Repton
for the Earl of Uxbridge.

BELSAY
Belsay, Northumberland
A splendid late-Picturesque garden
around the artificially ruinous
remains of the castle. The layout
immediately surrounding the fine
Greek-Revival house is from 1807,
overlaid by much later planting.

*BELTON
Belton, Lincolnshire
The very odd tower, and much of the
landscape, is by William Emes. An
amusing cascade and 'ruins'. Mostly
mid-period.

*BELVOIR CASTLE
Grantham, Leicestershire
Switzer worked on the grounds of the
earlier house. The present
spectacular pile is by Wyatt. Little
seems known about the park and
garden.

BENHAM PARK
Newbury, Berkshire
Another example of the
Brown/Holland partnership.

Antony House. *Above:* The view from the forecourt to the eye-catcher. (Some of the planting is modern.) *Below:* The east front.

Audley End: an elegant pavilion at the lake head.

Blaise: one of the charming cottages designed by Nash for the Picturesque village at Blaise. This one housed two families.

*BERRINGTON HALL
Leominster, Herefordshire
A pleasant example of a rather late park by Brown, dating from 1780.

*BICTON HOUSE
East Budleigh, Devonshire
A very late example of formalism, dating from 1735. The landscape movement hardly touched it. An arboretum was begun in 1830, and then everything much altered by Victorian owners.

BILSTON HOUSE
Bilston, Warwickshire
Of great interest because the estate was owned by Addison. He described the garden in an issue of the *Spectator* in 1712. Many changes since then, but a few elements from his time survive.

BISHOP'S PALACE
Bishop Auckland, Durham
A fine example of a deer house can be seen in the park.

BLAIR ADAM
Kelty, Fife
Owned by Robert Adam's family. A later owner published estate plans for 1733, 1748, 1792 and 1834. No gardens are shown in the first. There are formal ones in the second. The formalism has gone 'woolly' in the third and gone by the fourth. A fine kitchen garden remains by the house.

*BLAIR DRUMMOND
Stirling, Perthshire
The first naturalistic garden in Scotland, designed by Lord Kaimes between 1740 and 1750. Now a safari park.

*BLAISE CASTLE
Bristol, Avon
Marvellous late Georgian, a partnership between Nash and Repton. The latter's Red Book for the park and garden is dated 1796.

The Picturesque hamlet dates from fifteen years after.

*BLENHEIM PALACE
Woodstock, Oxfordshire
A magnificent place. The Loudon and Wise gardens contemporary with the house have all gone. However, Brown's £30,000 conversion has been immensely admired almost since its completion. There are some modern additions near the house.

*BLICKLING HALL
Blickling, Norfolk
Once away from the largely modern formality near the house, the park and lake are superb. Some good buildings, including a pyramid and a nice orangery. The woodland has some straight rides, probably from the early eighteenth century.

*BOUGHTON
Boughton, Northamptonshire
Although there was much done in the eighteenth century, the landscape style left the amazing formal system intact. It was probably too stupendous to suppress. It had 34,000 yards of clipped hedges, and several straight canals of three hundred yards long! A good late-Georgian Chinese tent can be found at the house, probably the only one left.

*BOWOOD
Calne, Wiltshire
A quite superb garden, with some poor modern intrusions. It was originally laid out with help from Charles Hamilton in the mid-century. It was then reworked by Brown, using all his typical elements. A village was cleared to make the lake, and much earth moved. Although not all Brown's plans were carried out, it was very chaste and much admired. Britton wrote in 1801: "In the grounds [there are] no

Blenheim Palace and the great bridge about which the Duchess of Marlborough was so angry. The canal beneath it was later turned into one of 'Capability' Brown's most beautiful lakes.

Blickling Hall seen across a small part of its vast lake. The sedges and water lilies would not have been allowed in the eighteenth century.

inanimate leaden statues, senseless busts nor ostentatious unmeaning obelisks."

BOYNTON HALL
Carnaby, Humberside
A good landscape, probably about 1770, with many buildings and bridges.

*BRAMHAM PARK
Leeds, West Yorkshire
Probably best placed in a book on formal gardens, although work was still in progress in the 1750s. To the north-east of the house is an interesting example of a 'clumped' avenue, so generally unsuccessful.

BREMHILL COURT
Bremhill, Wiltshire
A late attempt at a *ferme ornée*. The garden is dotted with suitable buildings.

BROCKLESBY HALL
Burton, Humberside
One of the few places that had a live hermit in the hermitage. He could, however unhappy, have looked out at a superb Brown landscape and even the Wyatt mausoleum and chapel. It had a much-admired kitchen garden, improved in the 1800s.

BROOKMANS PARK (GUBBINS)
Potters Bar, Hertfordshire
Once a famous early garden, originally by Bridgeman but landscaped when the estate absorbed a more famous park called 'Gubbins'. Little survives, and the house burned down in 1891.

*BROUGHTON HOUSE
Gatehouse, Kirkcudbrightshire.
The pleasure grounds were laid out by an otherwise little-known designer called Ramsay (not the painter) and are very attractive.

*BUCKLAND ABBEY
Tavistock, Devonshire
Sir Francis Drake's old estate. It once had a splendid formal layout, dating from the 1720s. William Marshall demolished it about 1780 and redesigned the park. He carved clumps out of the avenues and screens, finding it a very difficult commission.

*BURGHLEY HOUSE
Stamford, Cambridgeshire
Brown started here the year after he set up in practice, and continued working here for the next twenty-six years. Apart from making major alterations to the house, he demolished the surrounding terraces and created the present fine lake.

*BURTON CONSTABLE HALL
Hull, Humberside
The garden and lake are by White and date from the 1780s. There are several nice garden buildings. All this scarcely disguises the remains of a much earlier layout. Some of the avenues were 'clumped' into rather formal platoons. Interesting.

BUSRIDGE HOUSE
Busridge, Surrey
Some interesting buildings ranged along four lakes, with some very good planting and some nice walks.

CANONS
Edgware, Middlesex
The vanished formal splendours created for the Duke of Chandos still provoked fury among devotees of the landscape style long after the parterres had become fields. The canals survived for many years.

CARLTON HOUSE
London
A garden in almost continuous development from beginnings to

demolition. Before Brown redesigned it, there was a charming proto-landscape illustrated by Woollett in 1760.

CARSHALTON HOUSE
Carshalton, Greater London
The remains of a once-fine garden. Originally by Bridgeman, it then became a good proto-landscape, with canals and nice grottoes.

CASSIOBURY
Watford, Hertfordshire
It once had a very famous flower garden in the Chinese style and with Chinese plants. The house was demolished in 1922.

*CASTLE ASHBY
Wellingborough, Northants
A good lake and park by Brown.

*CASTLE HILL
South Molton, Devonshire
The gardens were once a fine example of very early landscaping. They survived until the nineteenth century, when much planting and re-planning were done.

*CASTLE HOWARD
Malton, Yorkshire
Very famous gardens indeed, and justly so. Most of it is before 1730, but the lakes date from the last years of the century. They were once formal fish-ponds.

CAVE CASTLE
South Cave, Yorkshire
An interesting example, now partly built over, of a small layout from the 1780s. It still has the usual fishing pavilions and ice-house, but the aviary has gone. Loudon thought it was very good indeed. It is now a country club.

CHARBOROUGH PARK
Morden, Dorset
A superbly planted park. Designer unknown.

*CHARLECOTE PARK
Stratford-upon-Avon, Warwickshire
A much earlier garden now invisible beneath Brown's alteration of the 1760s.

*CHATSWORTH
Chesterfield, Derbyshire
An absolutely splendid mixture of the seventeenth, eighteenth and nineteenth centuries. Most of the spectacular water is from the first period; the widened river and much of the planting is by Brown in the second; and many functional improvements are from the last. There were once some marvellous greenhouses by Paxton.

*CHILHAM CASTLE
Canterbury, Kent
An interesting layout. The formal elements near the house are probably original, surprisingly not swept away when the park was landscaped (and the lake formed) from 1777. Another Brown attribution.

*CHILLINGHAM CASTLE
Wooler, Northumberland
The remains of a good Georgian layout.

*CHILLINGTON HALL
Wolverhampton, Staffordshire
One of the largest and most impressive of Brown's gardens. Also some excellent garden buildings of the same period. However, the landscape has not obliterated what once must have been a fine formal garden.

*CHISWICK HOUSE
Chiswick, Greater London
The gardens were begun 1715–20 by Lord Burlington. Loudon said of them: "In the Italian style, with a redundancy of sculptural embellishment, but have since been

Vanbrugh's magnificent walk at Castle Howard, formally punctuated with statues, yet following the informal line of the old Henderskelf Lane. The lake is from later in the century; much of the planting is modern.

Claremont. *Above:* The 'landscaped' grounds before improvement by 'Capability' Brown, parts of which still exist. *Below:* The amphitheatre today. *Opposite above:* The Kentian island temple that can be seen, half hidden, in the painting above. *Opposite below:* The grotto at the head of the lake.

modernized." Described in Chapter 2, they are now being restored.

CIRENCESTER PARK
Cirencester, Gloucestershire
A very notable layout indeed. Partially described in the main part of the book, it has one of the earliest gothic follies (Alfred's Hall of 1721) and one of the earliest 'natural' lakes, (1735), the ends of which were concealed by plantations. This is twenty years earlier than anything by Brown.

*CLANDON PARK
West Clandon, Surrey
The grounds of this superb house are by Brown, commended by Loudon because "he transformed a chalk pit into a scene of Picturesque beauty". Brown also designed the fine stables. There is a fine grotto, containing a cold bath and statues.

*CLAREMONT
Esher, Surrey
Walpole's letter on the gardens is quoted on page 38. Brown demolished the house and gardens by Vanbrugh. Brown's layout was altered by Papworth. The kitchen gardens were admired as much as the landscape, especially for the elegant niches that sheltered the grape vines.

*CLAYDON HOUSE
Aylesbury, Buckinghamshire
The rather unexciting landscape is believed to have been designed by James Sanderson, of Caversham, between 1763 and 1776.

*CLEARWELL CASTLE
Monmouth, Gloucestershire
A late-Georgian 'castle' with the remains of a late-Georgian garden that was greatly admired.

*CLIVEDEN
Maidenhead, Buckinghamshire
A garden in an almost continuous state of change from the seventeenth to the early twentieth century. There are remains from almost all periods, including a 'Bridgemannic' theatre. The early-eighteenth-century wilderness was still in prime condition a hundred years later.

*CLUMBER PARK
Worksop, Nottinghamshire
Not a great deal seems known about this garden. Loudon much admired it. The house has gone, but there is still a splendid park and a large lake, and there was once a very good late-Georgian formal garden.

*COBHAM HALL
Cobham, Kent
The landscape is at least partly by Repton. Earlier than his alterations, it seems to have been fully baroque, with some marvellous avenues.

*CORBY CASTLE
Carlisle, Cumbria
A very picturesque garden indeed, with walks along a ravine and lots of statuary. All this is probably contemporary with the early-nineteenth-century additions to the house. Loudon suggests that this is one of the sites of very early landscape gardening, starting about 1706.

*CORSHAM COURT
Chippenham, Wiltshire
The early layout was by Keene, but Brown started work as architect and landscaper in 1761. He made the lake and planted many thousands of trees, including the fine cedars. The scheme was altered yet again by Repton in 1799, when the lake was enlarged, the clumps thinned and a lot of newly imported tree species planted. A new avenue was formed.

*COTEHELE HOUSE
Tavistock, Devonshire
The formality and the ancient oaks

Claydon House: the view across the lake.

Corsham Court, showing the 'Capability' Brown landscape (a typical example) just after its completion. It was altered soon after by Repton.

and chestnuts were much admired in the late-Georgian period, presaging the decline of interest in the landscape style.

COWESFIELD HOUSE

Downton, Wiltshire
In the early nineteenth century this was one of the few surviving *ferme ornées*, with ornamented hedges and turfed drives.

*CROOME COURT

Upton, Herefordshire
A splendid garden. The original and magnificent Jacobean house was sited on flat and marshy land. Brown, in his first major commission (1751), demolished the one and drained the other. The Earl of Coventry spent £40,000 on earth moving, a new house and garden buildings. Sanderson Miller advised. Robert Adam built a fine orangery. The first *Koelreuteria* and *Chimonanthus* were planted here in the 1760s. It was the last garden that Brown saw before he died.

*CROWCOMBE COURT

Taunton, Somerset
A superb landscape from 1725 to 1740. It is an early example of planting with native species only. A good gothic summerhouse is of rather later date.

*CULZEAN CASTLE

Ayr, Strathclyde
A superbly sited, and very beautiful, house. It was painted several times by Nasmyth, who may have advised on the garden design. There are dramatic cliff walks and fine kitchen and flower gardens. The avenue to the lake is now felled but is being replanted. A strange cliff-top lake, with a nice gothic summerhouse and aviary.

DALHOUSIE CASTLE

Edinburgh, Lothian
Now a hotel, the fine late-Georgian castellated house had a dramatic landscape garden, planned by John Hay, who did quite a number of Scottish gardens, as well as the kitchen garden at Alnwick. There was once a large collection of Canadian plants collected in that country by the Countess.

*DALKEITH PALACE

Edinburgh, Lothian
The estate is open, but little of what were once the most sumptuous gardens in the north remains. They once had fifty staff, a collection of a thousand species of herbaceous plants and a vast American collection. The pleasure gardens had fifty miles of walks. All of this is now forested. The kitchen gardens were immense and now contain a nursery garden.

DALMAHOY

Edinburgh, Lothian
A very good extant example of a 'Scottish park'. These were never for deer and were never conventionally landscaped. Straight belts surrounded the more or less rectangular paddocks and were for sheltering the cattle.

DALTON HALL

South Dalton, Yorkshire
An important survival of the early landscape style. A nice Palladian summerhouse by Colen Campbell also survives.

*DANSON PARK

Bexley, Kent
Loudon attributed the grounds to Brown.

*DEENE PARK

Corby, Northamptonshire
By 1746 the gardens had a single serpentine walk but were

Culzean Castle: the view north from the circular drawing-room of Robert Adam's
magnificent house. The gothic style overwhelms the classical; the natural landscape
overwhelms the garden.

Duncombe Park: one of the temples, *c.* 1720.

Fonthill Abbey: the Dell, with its lake just visible through the trees.

subsequently landscaped later in the century, and early in the next. A good lake and an interesting bridge.

DENTON MANOR
Denton, Lincolnshire
A good late-Georgian grotto by the side of an earlier lake. Probably somewhere are the bones of a good seventeenth-century layout.

*DITCHLEY PARK
Chipping Norton, Oxfordshire
Famous in the Georgian period for its ancient park with many narrow alleys and a five-mile avenue. The landscape must have been formed later.

*DODINGTON HOUSE
Bristol, Avon
Brown started various improvements from 1764. Two lakes were formed by damming the Frome. There is a curious serpentine aqueduct and a much-admired cascade. The various nineteenth-century additions include a fine curved conservatory.

DOWNTON CASTLE
Downton, Shropshire
Only the decayed remains of the famous estate survive. There were once walks along the rocky gorge, with grottoes along the way. The house was built in 1774, in 'serious' gothic.

DREGHORN CASTLE
Edinburgh, Lothian
The house is gone, and a barracks stand in the park. The layout of this was designed by Nasmyth in the early 1780s. An outer belt enclosed paddocks with scattered single trees. Much of the planting and some of the walks survive.

DROPMORE
Burnham, Buckinghamshire
See page 191. The house was built in 1790, but much added to. The

gardens were mostly laid out in 1810. They contained one of the finest collections of trees in Britain. Some garden buildings still exist, although the admired parterre has gone.

*DRUMMOND CASTLE
Crieff, Tayside
The gardens were much admired by Loudon. The parterre of 1820 remains.

DUDDINGSTON HOUSE
Edinburgh, Lothian
Golfers can walk round a Brown-style landscape by Robertson. The house, dating from about 1750, is by Chambers. Loudon thought it "bland and tame".

DUNCOMBE PARK
Helmsley, Yorkshire
An early and very important proto-landscape with a long curving terrace, terminated at each end with temples, one copied from Stowe. Much of the garden was formal, but the terrace was designed to get superb views of the surrounding country.

DUNGLASS HOUSE
Dunbar, Lothian
The house, now alas destroyed, was set on the edge of a spectacular ravine. The gardens were designed by Alexander Nasmyth and illustrated by Paul Sandby.

DUNMORE CASTLE
Stirling, Stirlingshire
Remarkable for one of the most astonishing of all garden buildings. The deservedly famous pineapple-shaped house is now restored.

*DYRHAM PARK
Bath, Avon
This once had a marvellous baroque garden lovingly described by Switzer, who may have helped with the

hydraulics. It was much altered during the landscape craze, and Repton may have had a hand. The deer park once contained five hundred acres.

EATON HALL
Eaton, Cheshire
The early nineteenth-century house replaced a much better one, perhaps by Vanbrugh. The extensive park was landscaped by Brown and then altered by Repton. Much of the second house is also gone.

ENDSLEIGH COTTAGE
Tavistock, Devonshire
A very grandiose *cottage ornée* built for the Duchess of Bedford. The house was by Wyattville, and there was a Repton garden to match. This had terraces edged with pretty railings, a smaller cottage in the Swiss style and much else. There was even to be a tiny cottage on the far side of the Tamar to improve and animate the view.

ENVILLE HALL
Enville, Staffordshire
A famous, much-visited and much-described garden in the Georgian period. Shenstone and Sanderson Miller did various buildings, and the former, helped by the Earl of Stanhope's brother, designed garden, park and lake. Only Shenstone was responsible for the cascade. Much is left, but all rather neglected.

ESHER
Esher, Greater London
One of William Kent's major proto-landscapes. The 1737 plan shows straight, and perhaps earlier, avenues, but with serpentine walks and most unusual zigzag ones as well, in the wildernesses in between the radials. Everything had vanished by 1829.

*EUSTON HALL
Thetford, Norfolk
Reasonably interesting. The bones of the garden were laid out by Evelyn, but there were many alterations by Kent, including some half-hearted clumps derided by Walpole, as "a dozen trees here and there, until a lawn looks like the ten of spades. Clumps have their beauty, but in a great extent of country. How trifling to scatter arbours, where you should spread forests."

EXTON PARK
Stratton, Leicestershire
The gardens have long been famous. The original Elizabethan house once had a garden with marvellous canals and cascades. They, and the rest of the layout, were by London and Wise. One of the last formal gardens made, they survived until the nineteenth century. Now all is landscape. There is a splendid gothic 'Fort Henry' by the lake.

FAIRFORD PARK
Cirencester, Gloucestershire
The park was designed by William Emes, surrounding an 'Athenian' Stuart house, later altered by Soane. Stuart did some of the temples.

FAWLEY COURT
Fawley, Buckinghamshire
An interesting garden, with a canal from the front of the house to the river. Maybe the same date as the garden buildings (mid-century).

*FELBRIGG HALL
Cromer, Norfolk
A fine and long-famous landscape. A good orangery.

FISHERWICK
Lichfield, Staffordshire
Once a flat site, Brown created hills and lakes and planted vast numbers of trees. All this was done from 1784. He did the house as well.

FONTHILL ABBEY
Hindon, Wiltshire
Only a fragment of William Beckford's vast house remains, and even smaller amounts of his father's Palladian mansion. From mid-century the gardens were vast and superb. Of these, much remains, including the remarkable entrance approach to the earlier house. The lake and much of the planting is superb. William did his own designs for the grounds by the Abbey. There were twenty-seven miles of rides, vast lawns, woodlands with the undergrowth composed of rare exotic and American species and allowed to grow wild. There was one of the first Alpine gardens in a quarry, a Norwegian garden with indigenous plants and buildings and an immense arboretum.

FOOTS CRAY PLACE
Footscray, Kent
A now-demolished copy of Palladio's Villa Rotonda (as is Mereworth Castle). The gardens were very plain and quite formal, surprising for the date of the house. The canals were admired.

FOXLEY
Hereford, Herefordshire
The estate was once owned by Uvedale Price and the subject of a marvellous painting by Gainsborough. The scene is suitably Picturesque. Most of it has vanished, the house going in 1950.

*FRAMPTON COURT
Frampton-on-Severn, Gloucestershire
More properly in a list of formal gardens, but it is a late example from the 1740s. The house and canal are fine, and the gothic garden-house is absolutely beautiful. Much modern planting.

*GIBSIDE HALL
Gateshead, Durham
Although the house is ruined, the gardens survive and are by Brown. Once four miles in circumference, there were some superb woods and avenues, and a chapel and orangery now being restored.

*GLYNDE PLACE
Lewes, Sussex
Loudon says: "Grounds much improved by the late Dr Trevor, but at present rather neglected."

*GODINTON PARK
Ashford, Kent
A fine layout dating from the eighteenth and early nineteenth century.

GOLDNEY
Bristol, Avon
Only occasionally open. A very rare and important example of a grandiose urban/suburban garden layout, being built from 1737 to 1764. Some splendid buildings, much modern planting but an absolutely magnificent grotto with water tumbling past statuary.

*GOODWOOD HOUSE
Chichester, West Sussex
Admired for the planting more than the design. The gardens had some of the first magnolias and cedars to be introduced.

GOPSALL HALL
Bosworth, Leicestershire
A now ruined house that was once moated. In the 1750s some stunning parterres remained, although the moat had been turned into a canal. The next decade saw everything altered, at a reputed cost of £100,000. This included a nice temple.

*GORHAMBURY HOUSE

St Albans, Hertfordshire
A nice classical house on an older
site. The ancient park of six hundred
acres was much admired.

GRIMSTHORPE CASTLE

Edinham, Lincolnshire
The park was once one of the largest
in the kingdom, there being a
hundred acres of lake and some
immense straight rides (from the
baroque garden); had all of Brown's
plans been carried out, the
assemblage would have been finer
than Blenheim.

*GRIMSTON GARTH

Heydon, Yorkshire
A superb baronial mansion,
surrounded by a park designed by
White, from 1784.

*GUNNERSBURY HOUSE

London
An interesting garden, although
much obscured by Victorian
additions. Loudon attributed the
basic garden to Kent and admired
the ancient cedars and the disposition
of the lakes. The gardens had early
examples of steam-heated glasshouses,
which were famous for their
pineapples. There was also a superb
collection of American trees.

HACKFALL

Ripon, Yorkshire
The grounds were much admired by
Gilpin. They had famous winding
walks along a spectacular gorge
which Loudon called "a singularly
romantic scene". The Victorians
loved it, too, but now many of the
trees are dead. Some good garden
buildings survive.

HACKWOOD PARK

Oldleasing, Hampshire
A good example of late eclecticism.
The hundred acres of pleasure

ground boasted an Italian garden
theatre and French formal gardens as
well as (earlier?) music temples and
an 'aquatic zoo'.

HAGLEY

Bromsgrove, Worcestershire
The house (by Sanderson Miller) was
surrounded by a very early and
famous landscape by the owner
George Lyttleton, a close friend of
Pope and Thomson. The woods were
filled with buildings, including
Stuart's Doric 'Temple of Theseus'.
Many buildings remain. When
Marshall visited it in the 1790s, the
inn was full of visitors seeing the
place. He thought the gardens were
becoming "seedy". By 1829 only
parts retained their original
character.

*HAREWOOD HOUSE

Leeds, Yorkshire
The grounds and lakes are by Brown,
from 1772 to 1782. Some
improvements were undertaken by
Repton at the turn of the century.

*HARTWELL HOUSE

Aylesbury, Buckinghamshire
A good eighteenth-century park, with
some nice garden buildings.

HAWKSTONE PARK

Whitchurch, Shropshire
One hopes that today's golfers
admire the landscape as much as the
late Georgians did. Most of the
improvements were carried out after
1780. There are some good lakes, a
marvellously labyrinthine grotto cut
into a cliff (once inhabited by a
hermit), a genuine castle and much
else.

HEMPSTEAD BURY

Hemel Hempstead, Hertfordshire
Loudon says that these gardens are in
transition between formal and
informal, so they may date from the
1730s.

Goldney: the grotto.

Holkham Hall: magnificent formality, with 'landscape' beyond the lodge.

*HEVENINGHAM HALL
Halesworth, Suffolk
The house rather overwhelms an appreciation of the grounds. Although much land has returned to agriculture, Brown's scheme can still be seen. The designs are still in the house. The kitchen gardens are interesting, with some original espaliered trees and a nice 'crinkum-crankum' wall dividing off the flower garden. There is a splendidly sited orangery by Wyatt and, far off across ploughed fields, a tiny temple. The terracing near the house is much later.

*HOLKHAM HALL
Holkham, Norfolk
A magnificent park. The scheme was started by Kent in 1729. He designed canals, pavilions and regimented bosquets (all now gone). The immense *Ilex* avenue dates from 1733. The place was not finished when Brown took over in 1762. At that date the tidal creek became a fine lake, and Kent's garden was partly demolished. Emes was employed from 1784, and he greatly enlarged the lake. Repton presented a Red Book in 1789, but it is not clear how many of his suggestions were followed. Loudon credits him with the design of an amusing ferry across the lake. In the early nineteenth century Kent's canals and pavilions were demolished, and some of the early planting thinned (most of this was done by the owner). Wyatt designed the nice orangery and many of the estate buildings. The terracing around the mansion is from later in the century and is the only blot on a superb scene.

HONINGTON HALL
Banbury, Oxfordshire
The landscape was designed by Sanderson Miller about 1755. His, too, were the garden buildings.

There is a charming painting of it by Thomas Robins, dated 1759.

*HOPETOUN HOUSE
Edinburgh, Lothian
Although the character of the house is mostly the result of Adam's work, the garden was not similarly remodelled. Much of it dates from 1735 to 1740 and was one of the last large formal gardens to be built in Scotland.

*HOUGHTON HALL
King's Lynn, Norfolk
Walpole believed the grounds to have been one of Kent's first designs, and as Houghton was owned by his father, he should have known. The grounds have recently been attributed to the house's architect (Colen Campbell) and Thomas Ripley. They are now superb.

*ICKWORTH
Bury St Edmunds, Suffolk
Quite an interesting garden, although the formal area behind the house dates from just after the close of the Georgian era. Long before the present house was completed, Brown had done landscaping (for Ickworth Lodge), between 1769 and 1776. A village was removed (only the church remains), and a now-vanished lake was created. The 'Albana Walk' may be his, and certainly it is most splendidly sited along the valley side. The park once contained eighteen hundred acres and was eleven miles in circumference.

*KEDLESTON HALL
Derby, Derbyshire
Although Adam did the house and some of the garden buildings, the grounds do not seem to be attributed to a designer of comparable stature. Loudon admired the "fine sheet of water, with cascades and islands, and a venerable group of oaks".

*KENWOOD
Highgate, Greater London
A nice layout, with lake and mock bridge. Some of the planting near the house is too late to be of interest. There used to be a famous American garden, where many of the species became naturalized.

*KEW
Kew, Greater London
The gardens have a past as illustrious as their present. Chambers did many garden buildings; the pagoda remains. The lake and the 'dell' were designed by Brown.

*KILLERTON
Exeter, Devonshire
The grounds were planted from 1820, and there is a good late-Georgian arboretum.

KING'S WESTON
Clifton, Gloucestershire
Now a college, the remains of the great Vanbrugh house once had a fine Brown landscape. There was an extensive American collection and a good flower and kitchen garden. There still are several fine garden buildings (including a lovely banqueting house) and the remains of formal canals of 1711. Loudon wrote of it: "The views, towards the Severn and the Avon, ravish the senses with their grandeur and beauty and render the place one of the finest in the county."

*KINMOUNT HOUSE
Annan, Dumfriesshire
A very romantic view was published in Neale's *Seats*. There are the remains of a remarkable formal scheme, with a good informal lake and rides. These are all shown on the first edition of the Ordnance Survey maps.

KIRTLINGTON PARK
Banbury, Oxfordshire
Brown's plans for the park still exist.

KNOWLE GRANGE
Sidmouth, Devon
A good late-Georgian garden with, unusually, a nice grotto. Sidmouth might reveal more examples of interest.

KYRE PARK
Tenbury, Worcestershire
The hospital grounds contain remnants of a good landscape dating from before 1756. The designer is unknown. It was admired by Loudon.

LANGLEY PARK
Maidstone, Kent
Repton's Red Book for this garden is owned by the RIBA. A most interesting scheme is suggested and was apparently carried out. The house was burned down in 1913.

THE LEASOWES
Halesowen, Shropshire
A most famous and influential garden, now vanished. It is described fairly fully in the text.

*LEEDS CASTLE
Maidstone, Kent
A superb castle in a lake and park supposedly by Brown.

LLANARTH HOUSE
Llanarth, Monmouthshire
A fine Nash house that had a garden designed by a gentleman named Lapidge, known for a few other gardens.

*LONGLEAT HOUSE
Warminster, Wiltshire
Brown, working here from 1757 to 1762, uncharacteristically left the seventeenth-century terracing near the house. However, all of London

Longleat, with its vast park sweeping almost up to the walls of the house.

Newstead Abbey, showing the lakeside forts from which Byron's father watched 'sea-battles'.

and Wise's early garden vanished. Much remains by Brown, although Repton made some alterations. The park was once fifteen miles in circumference.

*LOWTHER CASTLE
Lowther, Westmorland
Brown may have worked here. Loudon was very enthusiastic about it, saying that the vast park had a variety of scenery unsurpassed by anywhere else. The mile-long turfed terrace along the cliff-edge inspired Lord MacCartney to compare it with the gardens of the Emperor of China at Jehol. The house is now a shell.

LUSCOMBE CASTLE
Dawlish, Devonshire
An absolutely splendid Repton landscape, now fully mature. It was built for a member of the Hoare family, owners of Stourhead.

*LUTON HOO
Luton, Bedfordshire
One of the most admired of Brown's landscapes. It dates from 1764 to 1770. The fine natural site allowed Brown to make a good lake. The house is now much altered and slightly unbalances the composition.

*LYME PARK
Disley, Cheshire
A good mid-period landscape.

*MARGAM
Margam, Glamorganshire
The vast house was a ruin by the early nineteenth century, although the park and gardens were still maintained. The immense orangery of 1784 was said to contain some Elizabethan orange trees.

MEREWORTH CASTLE
Mereworth, Kent
One of the most beautiful houses anywhere. The gardens, sadly without the moat, retain part of a formal Palladian garden of which Lord Burlington would have disapproved.

MIDFORD CASTLE
Monkton Combe, Somerset
A lovely small park with a gothic teahouse of the 1780s.

*MILTON ABBEY
Milton Abbas, Dorset
Much visited in late-Georgian times, but mainly for the magnificent house by Chambers. This, once the village had been removed with some difficulty, soon had a fine landscape by Brown, although later altered by Repton. The nice folly was built from genuine gothic fragments of the ancient abbey demolished in the 1750s.

MOCCAS COURT
Longtown, Herefordshire
The owner of Hagley visited here in 1767 and admired the grounds more than his own. Brown was paid £100 for plans in 1778, but the scheme was eventually completed by the owner. It is still largely in original condition. There was once a splendid specimen of a 'weeping' oak that was very rare.

MOOR PARK
Rickmansworth, Hertfordshire
The gardens owned by the Countess of Bedford were copied at the other 'Moor Park' by Sir William Temple. Those here were demolished by Brown for Admiral Lord Anson, whose family also had Shugborough.

*MOOR PARK
Farnham, Surrey
Most traces of Sir William's garden have gone. Loudon thought it "a fine garden and very romantic".

*MOUNT EDGECUMBE
Plymouth, Devonshire
An ancient house and a spectacular

park. Many improvements were made by Earl Mount Edgecumbe in the early nineteenth century, and he published his own guide-book in 1821. It is now publicly owned.

*NEWBY HALL
Ripon, Yorkshire
The attractive gardens, admired by Loudon, date from the 1760s. The designer is unknown.

*NEWSTEAD ABBEY
Newstead, Nottinghamshire
A garden with many associations. Most of the tree-planting dates from the early nineteenth century, everything having been felled by Byron's spendthrift father. The same gentleman also had six boats on the lake. Battles were conducted from the amusing lakeside forts. There are a few remnants of the earlier baroque garden, especially a nice cascade.

*NOSTELL PRIORY
Pontefract, Yorkshire
Little seems known about the garden. The vast avenue is an unusual accompaniment to the lakes, bridge and summerhouse.

*NUNEHAM HOUSE
Nuneham Courtenay, Oxfordshire
The garden was mostly designed by the owner, Lord Harcourt, with assistance from Brown. Walpole described it in 1780 as "more Elysian than ever . . . one of the most beautiful landscapes in the world". Some of it still remains. Of Mason's famous flower garden, he said that it was "a quintessence of nosegays". By 1834 it was no longer fit for growing anything. It was restored and enlarged and very much altered in the 1900s, and now has an Italianate terrace.

OATLANDS
Weybridge, Surrey
Begun in 1747 by Kent. Wright designed the terrace and the river, as well as the walks and shrubberies. By 1759 it was famous enough to be illustrated. It included a grotto by Josiah Lane, one of the most marvellous ever built, but it was demolished in 1948.

OXTON HOUSE
Kenton, Devonshire
One of the first examples of the return to formalism, created at vast expense in the early 1800s. The vast naturalistic lake was preserved.

PAINSHILL
Cobham, Surrey
A most important garden, the trees now being felled and the buildings falling to ruin. The basic design was done by the Hon. Charles Hamilton, who held the lease from 1738 to 1773. He created the most stunning garden but went bankrupt doing it. Like William Beckford, he retired to Bath. The grounds still have many of his buildings, including the hermitage. The hermit, offered a contract of seven years for £700, lasted three weeks. The trees were grouped in a botanical way, and there were lavish plantings of the rarest species. Hamilton drank wine from his own grapes. Much of the present planting is by later owners, including Lord Carhampton, who closed the gardens to the public for the first time.

PARK PLACE
Remenham Hill, Berkshire
Owned by the same General Conway who had Temple Combe at Henley. There remains a Druids' Temple given to him by the people of Jersey, and various other pieces of garden architecture.

Painshill: a pre-war photograph of one of the nicest of all gothic pavilions. It is now in rather more disrepair.

PARLINGTON PARK
Tadcaster, Yorkshire
Although the house has gone, fragments of the immense garden design still exist, including the splendid triumphal arch. Traces of the parterre remained even after the landscape movement, as did the curiously regular 'clumped' remains of avenues and circles.

PAULTONS
Romsey, Hampshire
The house has now gone. Loudon attributed the layout to Brown; it may have been interesting, for a drawing in the RIBA collection shows the lake almost encircling the house.

PENICUIK HOUSE
Penicuik, Lothian
A much-studied example of an early Scottish landscape garden, designed by the owner, to principles he himself had laid down in doggerel verse. Now very romantic and overgrown.

*PENSHURST PLACE
Tunbridge Wells, Kent
Much admired by the late Georgians, especially for its ancient trees, although they mourned the park's reduction to a mere four hundred acres.

PEPER HARROW HOUSE
Peper Harrow, Surrey
Another example of a Brown garden surrounding a classical house by Chambers. Various later additions to both.

*PETWORTH HOUSE
Petworth, West Sussex
One of the first of Brown's commissions. Although he left the bones of the earlier baroque garden intact, there were vast amounts of earth-moving and planting. The clumps were originally composed just of oaks, beech and chestnut. The lake

was reputed to have cost £30,000. Everything still survives, although there is no longer the famous collection of oxen from all over the world. Five hundred deer are not sufficient recompense.

PIERCEFIELD (Persfield)
Chepstow, Monmouthshire
These once-splendid gardens were begun in 1740 and seem to have been an early example of those which took full advantage of the dramatic natural site and the views from it. It once had all the usual buildings, including a cold bath (how could they bear it?) on the gorge side. Marshall and Loudon admired it. Most of it is beneath a race-track and golf course.

*PLAS NEWYDD
Anglesey, Gwynedd
The house and estate were improved from the 1780s by Lord Uxbridge. Most of Repton's suggestions were carried out, including a very Brownian belt around the extended park. Much of this, and the scattering of single trees inside, has been obscured by later planting.

*PLAS NEWYDD
Llangollen, Denbigh
The residence of the famous 'Ladies of Llangollen'. A *cottage ornée* of which Loudon says: "an elegant residence fitted up in the cottage style" with a matching garden in the best taste.

*POLESDEN LACEY
Leatherhead, Surrey
A good late-Georgian house by Cubitt (1824), with fine contemporary grounds. Loudon was impressed by the long terrace.

*POLLOCK HOUSE
Glasgow, Strathclyde
The gardens of this splendid house show Scottish conservatism, being entirely formal.

Polesden Lacey: the recreated formality of the late-Georgian period.

Powis Castle: part of the splendid terracing, where planting is firmly subordinate to architecture.

*POWDERHAM CASTLE
Exeter, Devonshire
Open to the public in the eighteenth
and nineteenth centuries and much
admired. The park was ten miles in
circumference and had fine pleasure
grounds and kitchen garden.

*POWIS CASTLE
Welshpool, Powys
See text. A major garden in a fine
state of preservation.

*PRIOR PARK
Bath, Somerset
A very famous and much-illustrated
garden. Various designers did the
garden buildings, and Pope advised
generally, being a frequent guest.
The gardens have a splendidly sited
and very fine Palladian bridge of
about 1756. Little later alteration.

*RABY CASTLE
Staindrop, Durham
A marvellously theatrical gothic
house, with especially fine grounds.
It was once thought that "few places
in the empire [are] so magnificent".
An immensely long terrace is
interesting, as is the nice gothic
seat/pavilion.

RADWAY GRANGE
Banbury, Warwickshire
Sanderson Miller's own house. His
first gothic enterprise was Radway
Tower, built in 1747 to
commemorate the Battle of Edge-
hill. From that he went on to
grander things elsewhere, although
still finding time to add fountains
and cascades to his own grounds.

*RAGLEY HALL
Stratford-upon-Avon, Warwickshire
The gardens, once superb and
formal, were replaced by Brown with
the present layout.

*RIEVAULX TERRACE
Helmsley, North Yorkshire
A most romantic terrace curving
along the top of a steep hillside,
giving marvellous views of the Abbey
and the distant hills. One end is
terminated with a nice temple, the
other with a magnificent banqueting
pavilion. The whole assemblage has
been recently restored. It was built in
the late 1750s.

*RIPLEY CASTLE
Harrogate, North Yorkshire
The ancient house has a park and
pleasure ground by Brown, although
some of the planting near the house
is later.

*ROUSHAM
Steeple Aston, Oxfordshire
In 1737 work on the smallish
Bridgeman garden was nearly
complete. However, Kent took over
the following year (on advice from
Pope?) and erased almost everything.
The terraces to the south became
smooth lawns down to the river, and
elsewhere the garden was enlarged to
take in 'Praeneste' valley. Many
buildings, including a cold bath fed
by a strange sinuous stone rill, were
added. Walpole said of the whole
assemblage: "The garden is Daphne
in little; the sweetest little groves,
streams, glades, porticoes, cascades
and rivers imaginable. . . ." Pope
adored it. It is now very beautiful.

*RUDDING PARK
Harrogate, North Yorkshire
Visited by Repton in 1790, and a Red
Book was prepared. What was
actually carried out is uncertain.
Much of the planting and all of the
gardens near the house are modern
(and very fine).

*SALTRAM HOUSE
Plympton, Devonshire
Little seems known about the

233

Rievaulx Terrace: a view of
the Abbey ruins through
one of the gaps in the
planting.

Kent's 'Praeneste' at
Rousham.

gardens of this famous house. Loudon says that the newly completed approach was much admired, so the grounds were still being worked on in the 1820s.

ST PAUL'S WALDEN BURY
Hertfordshire
A very late and very handsome formal layout only finished in 1762. There is also an informal lake, with a temple by Chambers. The owners must have liked both styles. The gardens are splendidly maintained.

SCAMPSTON HALL
Thornton Dale, North Yorkshire
An interesting garden, with a number of nice buildings. One of these was once a deerfold with a gothic façade (there does not seem to have been any classical ones) and a Palladian bridge cheaply made of wood (possibly designed by Brown).

*SCOTNEY CASTLE
Lamberhurst, Kent
A rare and fine Picturesque landscape, the ancient moated castle left carefully ruined when the owners built themselves a crisp late-Georgian house higher up. It is all splendidly planted, but much of it is modern.

*SEZINCOTE
Moreton-in-the-Marsh, Gloucestershire
It would be difficult for any garden to compete with such a beautiful and exotic house. Much of the garden near the house is modern, but a number of 'Indian' architectural features remain, as do many of the original trees (mostly native species). Much of the garden design was by Daniell (who had produced many prints of India), with perhaps some help from Repton. Much of the actual planting was certainly designed by Daniell.

*SHEFFIELD PARK
Lewes, East Sussex
The amusing gothic house and its pleasure ground "in the best taste" are now in separate ownership. Brown created two fine lakes in the shallow valley, but these are now rather clogged with later and luxuriant planting.

*SHERBORNE CASTLE
Sherborne, Dorset
Pope knew this attractive garden when it still had formal canals and terraces, although the outermost parts had ancient groves with winding paths. Several buildings still associated with his frequent visits. Later, Brown removed much, created the recently restored lake and did much planting. There is an interesting orangery and a gothic dairy.

*SHERINGHAM HALL
Sheringham, Norfolk
Both house and garden are by Repton (1812–19). The garden is still more or less intact. Much later planting.

SHOTOVER
Bullingdon, Oxfordshire
Although Kent designed an obelisk and a temple for the gardens in 1730, the landscape never took over, and there are good remains of the formal layout of 1718.

*SHUGBOROUGH
Stafford, Staffordshire
An interesting garden, much reduced in extent after 1795. The original mid-century layout was crammed with bridges, ruins, classical buildings (including the lovely Temple of the Winds) and a Chinese pavilion of 1747 which can hardly have convinced Admiral Anson of its authenticity. The River Trent flooded the garden in 1795, and this

The handsome, solid-roofed orangery at Sherborne Castle.

Shugborough Hall: 'The Temple of the Winds' by George 'Athenian' Stuart.

Shugborough: the 'ruins' survived the re-landscaping at the end of the eighteenth century.

was taken as an excuse to return much of the land to agriculture. Re-landscaping was carried out by John Webb up to 1805. Samuel Wyatt designed the fine farmhouses and cottages.

*SLEDMERE HOUSE
Norton, North Yorkshire
Loudon thought the house and grounds very elegant. The latter were laid out by Brown.

*SOUTHGATE GROVE
Southgate, Greater London
Loudon much admired the Repton park, saying that it was the finest in the county. It is now public. The house is by Nash.

*SOUTHILL PARK
Bedford, Bedfordshire
The old formal gardens survived until Henry Holland came to redesign it in 1803. There is a charming fishing pavilion of 1807.

*SPETCHLEY PARK
Spetchley, Hertfordshire
The earlier garden was described by Evelyn. It is now a splendid eighteenth-century park, with many buildings from that date.

*SQUERRYES COURT
Sevenoaks, Kent
The house is late seventeenth century, with gardens to match. However, the avenues have been 'clumped', and the lake and terraces are from the following century.

STACKPOLE COURT
Pembroke, Pembrokeshire
It was here that the monster pineapple of 1821 was grown. However, it was not only the glass that was superb: the park and grounds were magnificent.

*STOURHEAD HOUSE
Wincanton, Wiltshire
In spite of the blaze of rhododendrons and azaleas, and the loss of some of the garden buildings, this is one of the most perfect and serene gardens anywhere. Most of the construction was done between 1740 and 1760. The lake and the marvellous Pantheon were done exactly in the middle of the period. The layout was planned by the banker Henry Hoare; most of the buildings were designed by Henry Flitcroft. It was much visited from the time of its completion, and an inn had to be specially built for tourists. The gravel paths date from 1783. The garden must have been even more Arcadian without them. Some areas are still not open to the public.

*STOWE HOUSE
Buckingham, Buckinghamshire
Probably the most influential Georgian garden of all. It developed continuously between 1713 and 1776, a few years before the death of its second owner. Fourteen garden buildings have vanished, but thirty-seven remain. Only architectural historians will regret the loss. Bridgeman and Vanbrugh worked here before 1730, and even in 1722 it was the finest seat in England. At that time there were only twenty-eight acres of garden, enclosed by the sort of mock fortifications that were copied elsewhere. Kent worked on the area called "the Elysian Fields". Later, Brown smoothed out the ramps, turfed over the gravel walks and removed all remaining formal elements. Everyone visited it; Walpole was more awed by that fact than by the garden's beauty. In 1783 Marshall thought that there were far too many buildings. It was all Art and no Nature.

Stourhead House. *Above left:* The Pantheon, *c.* 1750, by Flitcroft. It contains various pieces of sculpture, including a 'Hercules' by Rysbrack. *Above right:* The River God in the grotto. *Below:* A general view of the bridge, lake and Pantheon. The grotto can be seen on the far right.

*STRAWBERRY HILL

Twickenham, Greater London
See text. Walpole wrote, in one of his letters:

> I am just come out of the garden, in the most oriental of all evenings, and from breathing odours beyond those of Araby. The acacias . . . are covered with blossoms, the honeysuckles dangle from every tree in festoons, the seringas [*sic*] are thickets of sweets, and the new cut hay in the field, tempers the balmy gales . . . while a thousand sky rockets, launched in the air at Ranelagh and Marlebone [*sic*], . . . give it the air of Haround Alrachid's Paradise.

The less romantic Loudon said that "the grounds are of very limited extent, and much less interesting than has been generally imagined; without the Thames, they would be nothing."

*STUDLEY ROYAL

Studley Roger, North Yorkshire
Notable not only because of their astonishing beauty but because Fountains Abbey was added to the garden only in 1768, and also because the original owner had the good sense to refuse Brown's offer to landscape the garden. The gardens were begun in 1720 and ten years later were "the wonder of the north". Formalism and the natural landscape are wonderfully contrasted. There are some nice pavilions. When Loudon described them, they were becoming decrepit. They are now in fine order; the house was demolished in 1946.

*SYON HOUSE

Greater London
The garden and park have been in more or less continuous change since the sixteenth century. Most of the present layout results from Brown's work here, and there is a fine and unaltered lake on the north side. Many improvements date from the 1820s, especially the magnificent suite of glass. Loudon was pleased that some of it was curvilinear.

*TATTON PARK

Knutsford, Cheshire
Once the visitor has got away from the much-altered gardens near the house, he will find an immense Repton park, with a vast and splendid lake. There is some later planting, especially of rhododendrons. The kitchen garden was once superb (with a good pinery). The flower garden once had the only example I have come across of a moss border. Very advanced.

TAYMOUTH CASTLE

Kenmore, Perthshire
The early house once had sumptuous formal gardens, but alterations began in the 1730s. The house was rebuilt and in 1792 had rather Stowe-like gardens, with terraces and walks terminating in temples and forts. Many garden buildings survive. Marshall did some landscaping in the 1790s, and Nasmyth may have advised early in the next century. He certainly designed a bridge and a fort in 1816. The estate was vast, and Marshall thought it approached the Sublime.

*TEMPLE NEWSAM

Leeds, West Yorkshire
A good layout, with formal bones of 1712 still showing, but the landscaping 'flesh' attributed to Brown.

THICKET PRIORY

East Cottingwith, Yorkshire
The park (still extant) once showed a superb example of an early landscape garden. There still is an interesting curved lake.

Stowe. *Above:* The Palladian bridge, one of the many surviving garden buildings.
Below: 'The Shepherd's Rest', a hermitage.

Studley Royal: one of the many charming pavilions scattered along the curious formal–informal design.

Tatton Park: the Broad Walk.

THORESBY
Worksop, Nottingham
The formal gardens survived until
1756. They were then landscaped,
over a number of years, by
Richardson. None of this lasted long,
for it was replaced by formality early
in the nineteenth century in the
French style. The old house also
went, the present one being by
Salvin. There are some interesting
drawings in the RIBA collection
relating to the conversion of a formal
bason to an informal lake, at a cost of
£409. 12s. 6d.

TONG CASTLE
Wolverhampton, Shropshire
The house was demolished in 1954.
Both it and the park were once
attributed to Brown, but at least the
house was by another hand. It dates
from 1765. The park was splendid,
with a marvellous gothic garden
house and an unusually late example
(1822) of a hermitage with a live
hermit.

*TONG HALL
Bradford, West Yorkshire
The park probably dates from the
1770s, the same years that saw the
alterations to the house.

TOTTENHAM HOUSE
Savernake, Wiltshire
The grounds have a very rare
example of Lord Burlington's work
(a pavilion). Presumably the layout
would originally have been in the
Chiswick manner, but it is now by
Brown.

*TREDEGAR HOUSE
Abergavenny, Monmouthshire
A fine eighteenth-century park, with
a number of ancient trees that pre-
date it.

*TRENTHAM
Trentham, Staffordshire

Now largely a Victorian garden, but
there is a Brown landscape
underneath, and the mile-long lake
still exists.

TRING
Tring, Hertfordshire
A delightful eighteenth-century park
by an unknown designer, now with a
by-pass through it. Some of the
clumps look as if they have been part
of an earlier formal layout.

TWICKENHAM
Pope's Villa, Twickenham, Middlesex
See text. The grotto still exists, if in a
rather sorry state. The obelisk went
to Penn House, and no trace of the
vineyard or the kitchen garden
remains.

*UPPARK
Petersfield, West Sussex
Repton altered the marvellous house
to take advantage of the view and of
his new landscaped gardens. The Kip
view suggests that the changes should
be regretted.

VALLEYFIELD
Culross, Fife
Only a few sagging walls remain of
the once-famous garden. In addition
to the good mid-Georgian layout was
the flower garden that was Repton's
only Scottish commission (see page
87).

WAKEFIELD LODGE
Towcester, Northamptonshire
There is little left of the layouts
designed by Kent and Brown. Kent
was here from the 1740s and thinned
out the ancient forest. A sloping lawn
was made to the north of the pond
and planted with his usual clumps.
Little is known of Brown's work.

*WANSTEAD PARK
Wanstead, Greater London
The house, a vast and magnificent

Wardour Castle. *Above:* Wardour Castle was kept as a picturesque ruin, near which was built a splendid grotto and a gothic pavilion by the lake. *Below:* The grotto.

one of 1715, and its London and Wise grounds were sold off in lots in the 1820s. By that time, one of the canals had become a lake that can still be seen in the park. There is also a nice grotto. There was once an American garden that was much admired.

*WARDOUR CASTLE
Tisbury, Wiltshire
The magnificent old castle was left as an authentic ruin and stands mocking the little gothic dining pavilion and the splendid grotto by Josiah Lane. All overlook the now rather overgrown lake. A lovely place. There are plenty of other garden buildings and, of course, the superb house. Brown's name has been associated with the grounds near that.

*WARWICK CASTLE
Warwick, Warwickshire.
A small and very early example of a garden by Brown, done for Lord Brooke before Brown set up in practice. There are some later additions.

*WELBECK ABBEY
Worksop, Nottinghamshire
One of the first large-scale jobs by Repton. Many avenues vanished or were clumped. There were radical alterations to the house.

WENTWORTH WOODHOUSE
Rotherham, Yorkshire
The house has always rather overwhelmed the ground, for it is two hundred yards long and covers three acres. The park was vast, covering fifteen hundred acres, and there was a large lake. Repton worked there from 1790.

*WEST WYCOMBE PARK
West Wycombe, Buckinghamshire
A marvellous house in marvellous gardens. Both developed together. The garden was begun by the owner, Sir Francis Dashwood, although he may perhaps just have fiddled about with an earlier formal scheme, of which the Broad Walk survives. From 1752 he was helped by Jolivet, who kept most of the formality but added serpentine walks and informal lakes. After 1770 a pupil of Brown's, called Thomas Cook, assisted. Dashwood was fascinated by architecture, and so the garden was heavily loaded with buildings. The lake had a large number of boats. The whole scheme was thinned out by Repton to nearly its present form. The garden has always been famous, and there are many prints and paintings of it.

*WESTON PARK
Newport, Staffordshire
A fine garden by Brown (from 1762), with two lakes and a nice temple and orangery. South of the house there are some Victorian additions. There is a magnificent kitchen garden.

WHITTON
Hounslow, Greater London
An interesting place, and a sad loss. The house was originally a sort of residential orangery built for the Duke of Argyll. It was sold in 1766, when it was still set in a fine proto-landscape, with wilderness and serpentine walks. The gardener had been James Lee, who set up the famous nursery of Lee and Kennedy. The house was demolished, and the new, and elegant, villa was soon bought by Sir William Chambers.

*WIDDICOMBE HOUSE
Salcombe, Devonshire
An interesting Georgian house, with grounds by Brown.

WILLINGHAM HOUSE
Ringmer, East Sussex

The grounds have a quite rare example (for Britain) of a combined grotto and gazebo.

*WILTON HOUSE

Wilton, Wiltshire
The superb house once had an equally fine Jacobean garden, but the grounds were landscaped in the 1730s by the owner. There may have been a little help from Kent. The river has the most superb Palladian bridge in the country. On the hillside beyond it can be seen a nice little temple by Chambers.

WIMPOLE HALL

New Wimpole, Cambridgeshire
The gardens have a nice gothic castle by Sanderson Miller.

*WOBURN ABBEY

Woburn, Bedfordshire
Ancient gardens, now most strongly flavoured by the late-Georgian period. An intermediate layout, and much planting, was done by Philip Miller. Repton worked here from 1806, adding many new elements (see text). Holland designed the Chinese dairy, and the interior was done by Crace. Both are good.

WOBURN FARM

Chertsey, Surrey
Vanished by 1829. See text.

WORMLEYBURY

Wormley, Hertfordshire
The nice park, with its lake, once contained a very famous collection of Chinese and Indian plants.

*WOTTON HOUSE

Aylesbury, Buckinghamshire
A nice early-Georgian house set in grounds by Brown.

WORKSOP MANOR

Worksop, Nottinghamshire
This once-gigantic house, of 1761, had an immense and earlier proto-landscape of the 1730s. Pieces of this remain; a hemicycle, some bridges and an island with an unusual ziggurat or mount. A later wave of landscaping seems to have been undertaken in the 1760s.

*WREST PARK

Wrest, Bedfordshire
A splendid and interesting garden. Much mid-nineteenth-century work, but part of the garden is an early work by Brown. However, the most important aspect of the grounds is the baroque layout, which has some fine canals and the marvellous pavilion by Archer.

WROXTON ABBEY

Wroxton, Oxfordshire.
Although much has gone, there are remains of the 1728 scheme by Bobart and of the landscape designed by the owner (Lord North) between 1733 and 1748. There are two nice lakes joined by a cascade, and a good serpentine 'river'.

WYNNSTAY

Ruabon, Denbighshire
Attributed to Brown, the cascade may date from an earlier garden. It was at this seat that bananas were first brought to fruit under glass.

Wilton: the Palladian bridge.

Woburn Abbey: the Chinese dairy was once surrounded by plants from China.

Bibliography: Contemporary sources

AITON, WILLIAM: *Hortus Kewensis etc.* (1810–13)

BRADLEY, RICHARD: *A Survey of the Ancient Husbandry and Gardening, etc.* (1725).

BRAYLEY, EDWARD and BRITTON, JOHN: *The beauties of England and Wales* (1801–15).

BURKE, EDMUND: *A Philosophical Enquiry into the Origin of our Ideas of the Sublime and Beautiful* (1757).

CASTELL, ROBERT: *The Villas of the Ancients* (1728).

CHAMBERS, SIR WILLIAM: *A Dissertation on Oriental Gardening* (1772).

COBBETT, WILLIAM: *The American Gardener* (1821).

DODSLEY, ROBERT and JAMES: *London and its environs described* (1761).

FALCONER, WILLIAM: *An historical view of the Taste for Gardening* (1783)

GILPIN, WILLIAM: *Three essays on picturesque beauty, etc.* (1794)

HILL, SIR JOHN: *Eden; or a Complete Body of Gardening* (1757)

JACKSON, MARIA: *The Florist's Manual, etc.* (1822)

JOHNSON, GEORGE W.: *The History of English Gardening* (1822)

JUSTICE, JAMES: *The Scots gardeners director* (1754)

KIP, JAN AND KYNFF, LEONARD: *Britannia Illustrata* (1709)

KRAFFT, JOHN: *Plans des plus beaux jardins, etc.* (1810)

LANGLEY, BATTY: *New Principles of Gardening* (1728)

LOUDON, JOHN C.: *Encyclopaedia of Gardening* (1822)

MARSHALL, WILLIAM: *Planting and Rural Ornament* (1785)

MASON, WILLIAM: *An Heroic Epistle to Sir William Chambers* (1777)

MASON, WILLIAM: *The English Garden* (1783)

MAWE, THOMAS: *Everyman his own gardener* (by J. Abercrombie) (1767)

MILLER, PHILIP: *The Gardeners' Dictionary, etc.* (from 1731)

MORRIS, RICHARD: *Flora Conspicua* (1826)

NEALE, JOHN P.: *Views of the Seats of Noblemen and Gentlemen* (1824)

NEILL, PATRICK: *Scottish gardens and orchards* (1813)

NICOL, WILLIAM: *The Villa Garden Directory* (1809)

PAPWORTH, JOHN B.: *Rural residences, etc.* (1818)

PAPWORTH, JOHN B.: *Hints on Ornamental Gardening* (1823)

PHILLIPS, HENRY: *Flora Historica, or the three seasons* (1824)

PHILLIPS, HENRY: *Floral Emblems* (1825)

PRICE, UVEDALE: *Essays on the Picturesque* (1810)

REPTON, HUMPHREY: *Sketches and Hints on Landscape Gardening* (1794)

REPTON, HUMPHREY: *Observations on the theory and practice of landscape design* (1803)

REPTON, HUMPHREY: *An enquiry into the changes of taste in landscape gardening* (1806)

REPTON, HUMPHREY: *Fragments of theory and practice of landscape gardening* (1816)

SERLE, JOHN: *A plan of Mr Pope's garden* (1745)

SHAW, JAMES: *Plans of Forcing-Houses in Gardening* (1794)

SWITZER, STEPHEN: *Ichnographia Rustica, etc.* (1718)

TEMPLE, SIR WILLIAM: *Upon the Gardens of Epicurus* in collected works Volume I, *Miscellanea*

TRUSELER, JOHN: *The Elements of Modern Gardening* (1784)

WALPOLE, HORACE: *A History of the Modern Taste in Gardening* in *Anecdotes on Painting* (1780)

WHATELY, THOMAS: *Observations on Modern Gardening and laying out of pleasure grounds, etc.* (1770)

Bibliography: Post-Georgian sources

ALLEN, BEVERLEY: *Tides in English taste, 1619–1800* (1937)

AMHERST, ALICIA: *London's parks and gardens* (1907)

BROCKMAN, H.: *The caliph of Fonthill* (1956)

CHASE, ISABEL: *Horace Walpole: Gardenist* (1943)

CLARK, KENNETH: *The Gothic Revival* (1928)

CLARK, KENNETH: *Landscape into Art* (1949)

CLIFFORD, DEREK: *The history of garden design* (1962)

GREAN, STANLEY: *Shaftesbury's philosophy of religion and ethics* (1967)

GLOAG, JOHN: *Loudon's England* (1970)

HADFIELD, MILES: *Landscape with trees* (1967)

HONOUR, HUGH: *Chinoiserie* (1961)

HYAMS, EDWARD: *Capability Brown and Humphrey Repton* (1971)

HUNT, JOHN D.: *Emblem and expressionism in the eighteenth-century landscape*, in *Eighteenth-Century Studies*, iv, 294–317

HUNT, JOHN D. and WILLIS, PETER: *The Genius of the Place* (1976)

HUSSEY, CHRISTOPHER: *The picturesque; studies in a point of view* (1927)

HUSSEY, CHRISTOPHER: *English gardens and landscapes, 1700–1750* (1967)

JOURDAIN, MARGARET: *The works of William Kent* (1948)

MANWARING, ELIZABETH: *Italian landscape in the eighteenth century England* (1925)

MALINS, EDWARD: *English landscape and literature, 1660–1840* (1966)

MORDAUNT-CROOK, J.: *The Greek revival* (1972)

OWEN, JOHN B.: *The Eighteenth Century, 1714–1815*

STROUD, DOROTHY: *Capability Brown* (1957)
Humphry Repton (1962)

SUTTON, DENYS: "Gaspard Dughet", in *Scottish Art Review*, Volume 10, no. 4; 4–7

WATKIN, DAVID: *Thomas Hope and the Neo-Classical Idea* (1968)

WITTKOWER, RUDOLPH: *Palladio and English Palladianism* (1974)

WOODBRIDGE, KENNETH: *Landscape and antiquity; aspects of English culture at Stourhead, 1718–1838.* (1970)

Index

252

253

254